Global
Education

From Thought
to Action

**1991 Yearbook of the
Association for Supervision
and Curriculum Development**

Edited by Kenneth A. Tye

Developing Leadership for Quality in Education for All Students

Printed in the United States of America. Typeset on Xerox™ Ventura Publisher 2.0. Printed by Edwards Brothers.

Ronald S. Brandt, *Executive Editor*
Nancy Modrak, *Managing Editor, Books*
Carolyn R. Pool, *Associate Editor*
Lars Kongshem, *Editorial Assistant*
Stephanie Kenworthy, *Assistant Manager, Production Services*
Valerie Sprague, *Desktop Specialist*
Al Way, *Manager, Design Services*

$19.95
ASCD Stock No. Y9100
ISBN: 0-87120-171-2

Library of Congress Catalogue Card No. 44–6213 (ISSN 1042–9018)

Global Education: From Thought to Action

Foreword

My career in education began in the early 1960s and spanned the years when the United States was more powerful than any of its global neighbors, economically, politically, industrially, and technologically—the hegemony years. During that time, I successfully taught and administered as I had been taught, with a brand of U.S. ethnocentricity that would have made any patriot proud. I learned and fostered the notion that anything not American—anything different—was by definition deficient. I questioned the deficit-difference philosophy only from an inter-U.S. perspective when it was misapplied to describe gender, religious, or racial differences. I accepted the paternalistic mantle with pride because I believed that the United States had the best solutions to the world's problems.

In reality, the United States did provide other nations with assistance during their development, albeit inextricably interlocking their destiny with ours; but that was then, and this is now. While still intensely patriotic, we are no longer paternalistic. We as a nation understand the necessity for responsible global citizenry; yet most schools in America do not prepare students to assume that responsibility. We recognize that the world's people have common needs and wants, but we as yet do not consider the many different perspectives on how to share in the world's resources. Without global education, we may never be exposed to these differing perspectives.

In the face of extensive economic, technological, and political changes, we must learn more about the economics, education, environmental conditions, cultures, and technologies of our global neighbors and how our decisions affect each other. The multidimensional quality of each issue demands that we consider the perspective of those indigenous to the cultures of all stakeholders, understanding that a specific point of view is often shaped by the viewing point. We must accept the interrelationship of our futures and share the responsibility to prepare students to critically assess information gathered across time and cultures as they craft new world policies for times to come.

I commend the membership of the Association for Supervision and Curriculum Development for demonstrating leadership in education by establishing global understanding as a focus area, and I thank the authors of this book for illuminating the issues.

DONNA JEAN CARTER
ASCD President, 1990–91

Introduction: The World at a Crossroads

Kenneth A. Tye

*T*he United States—indeed, the world—is at a quite critical cross-roads. In every direction are new economic, political, cultural, ecological, and technological realities that are sometimes astounding, such as the opening of the Berlin Wall and the wave of democracy in Eastern Europe. In the 1990s, our populace and leaders will need attitudes and behaviors that recognize and promote interdependence and cooperation among nations. However, getting this fact understood in a society based on individualism and competition is not easy. As we have been told by social scientists, Americans have a deep desire for autonomy and self-reliance (Bellah et al. 1985). We are a nation founded in independence. Separateness is a cultural norm for us. Our heroes are lonesome cowboys and hard-boiled detectives who work by themselves. Our economic system is based on individual enterprise, entrepreneurship, and competition. In the workplace, the goal is to "get to the top," despite our understanding that "it is lonely at the top." For Americans, changing our attitudes and behaviors so that our society will be able to adapt and survive will indeed be challenging.

The schools have a major role to play in this process of adaptation, and global education is a movement that holds much promise as a facilitating force. Although there is a growing number of global education projects across the United States, many educators and most lay people understand neither the need for global education nor its promise. In fact, many people are frightened by the changes occurring in the world; they seem to distrust even the term *global education.*

Given this situation, the authors of ASCD's *1991 Yearbook* have set out to accomplish three purposes. The first two are straightforward: (1) to explain, as clearly as possible, what global education is and why it is particularly important in our schools at present and (2) to assist those who wish to develop their own

1

global education program by describing how it works and how it can be implemented.

The third purpose of the yearbook is more complex. We see global education as a movement with the potential for promoting in our schools many of the improvements that thoughtful people (such as the membership of the Association for Supervision and Curriculum Development [ASCD]) have sought throughout this century. Some of these improvements have proven elusive—for example, interdisciplinary planning and teaching, the development of critical thinking abilities, the use of the community as a learning laboratory, cooperative learning, and intrinsic motivation of student learning. We hope to show how global education can serve as a vehicle for bringing about school improvement.

The Network Project

Barbara Tye and I serve as co-directors of the Center for Human Interdependence (CHI) and the Network Project, both associated with Chapman College, Orange County, California. Previously, we both were part of John Goodlad's team at the Research Division of the Institute for Development of Educational Activities (I/D/E/A) in Los Angeles. At I/D/E/A and in other contexts, Barbara and I have had a good deal of experience with both global education and school change. Because of our background, the CHI Network Project operated with the following assumptions:

1. The school is the optimal unit on which to focus educational change efforts. While the facilitating behaviors of superordinate agencies (e.g., district and state) and individual classroom teachers are important, what is most critical is to get concerted action at the local school site.

2. Lasting school improvement will come through the facilitation of teacher and school action. The mandating of new programs from superordinate levels, in reality, impedes school improvement (see Chapter 2 for an elaboration of these assumptions).

Given these assumptions, in 1985 CHI put together a network of 11 schools (3 high schools, 4 middle schools, and 4 elementary schools) in eight school districts in Orange and southern Los Angeles Counties in California. The criteria for inclusion were simply that (1) the superintendent, principal, and a significant number of teachers (purposely never precisely defined, but ranging from 10 to 50 percent) had to agree to participate, and (2) the district had to provide 10 to 15 days of teacher release time for use by each school involved in the project.

The activities of the project are fully described in a forthcoming book (B. Tye and K. Tye in press). It is adequate to state here that nothing was imposed on the participating teachers. Instead, we began by asking them what they were interested in doing. CHI staff members visited the schools and provided instructional materials, consultants, and ideas as the need for such resources was identified by teachers, administrators, and support personnel. Small grants (approximately $600 each) were offered, no strings attached, to teachers and others with ideas about how to globalize the curriculum. Proposals were judged by CHI staff and a panel of project participants. Networkwide activities (workshops, conferences, and special projects) brought staff members from various schools together for workshops on common interests, such as global economics, folklore and folk art, environmental issues, and conflict resolution, as well as how to teach controversial issues. CHI regularly published a newsletter featuring school activities, global education concepts, and practical lessons. In addition, special projects involved segments of the network. Four schools had international telecommunications connections, middle school students from several schools gathered for an international sports day at which the students played noncompetitive games from other countries, and volunteer teachers from several schools participated in a special community-related project called "Orange County in the World." This project was modeled after the Columbus in the World program developed by the Mershon Center at Ohio State University (Alger 1974).

All of this activity was designed as part of a field study to answer the question, "What does it take to bring a global perspective to the curriculum of a school?"

We employed qualitative, field study methodologies in an attempt to develop what Glaser and Strauss (1967) call "grounded theory." Further, though we were not totally limited to one perspective, we were heavily influenced by Herbert Blumer (1969) and other symbolic interactionists. Simply put, we were mostly interested in the meaning people gave to their experience.

Each CHI staff member fully documented every contact with network members by taking observation notes, as well as theoretical notes. The former reflected on ways in which we were conducting our study; the latter, on conceptual issues arising from our work. Periodically, staff members prepared memos that pulled together a person's thinking about given concepts.

We met as a team frequently to discuss and reflect on our findings. Often, a memo served as the beginning point of a discussion. The usual outcome of such a meeting was the raising of further questions, which became the focus of subsequent observations and interviews. The process was one of data gathering, reflection, further data gathering, and so on.

Beginnings of a Dialogue

In June 1988, at the Pacific Rim Conference in Vancouver, British Columbia, Barbara and I made a brief presentation about the CHI project. We gave an overview and then shared some preliminary findings.

At the end of our session, Jan Tucker, who was completing his term as President of the National Council for the Social Studies and who directs his own global education project in Florida, encouraged us in our view that the global education movement could well benefit from paying closer attention to the literature on school change. As I recall, we briefly discussed the possibility of getting a few people together to explore that idea.

At the conclusion of the conference, Barbara and I traveled by car into the forests and mountains of British Columbia. Somewhere on the Duffy Lake Road, in magnificent surroundings, the idea came to us that we should organize such a dialogue. Further, we thought we could facilitate such a discussion by focusing it on the data we were collecting in our study of school-based global education projects. Finally, it occurred to us that such an event might result in a quite significant publication.

We finished our vacation in Western Canada and returned home to Southern California refreshed. Sometime in early fall of 1988, I began in earnest to pursue the idea of a dialogue on global education and school change. I called the people who eventually became the authors of this yearbook and proposed a weekend meeting early in 1989. I was pleasantly surprised to find that everyone contacted enthusiastically endorsed the idea.

Monograph Weekend

In mid-January 1989, the ten authors of this book, along with other CHI staff members, gathered at CHI. Barbara briefly discussed the Global Education Network Project and the school intervention strategies that were being employed.

At the Friday evening meeting of what came to be called the "monograph weekend," Roberta Lessor, a sociologist colleague of ours at Chapman College and consultant to the Network Project, explained our research design and activity. That, too, is more fully described in the forthcoming book (B. Tye and K. Tye in press).

On Saturday morning, authors were immersed in data. We had on hand separate files for each of the 11 schools; each file contained field notes, memos, end-of-year reports, class observation notes, grant project reports, special interview data, newsletter articles, class and teacher schedules, and any other materials from or about the school. In addition, a 12th file contained cross- and between-school data, such as notices and correspondence to principals; annual reports to the Helen Devitt Jones Foundation, our major fundor; and workshop evaluations.

By the end of the weekend, we had a final outline, resulting from our examination of the data and the personal interests and experiences of the authors, that ultimately led to the content for this book. Chapter 2 was added later.

A growing number of individuals are involved in global education. Many of them would have been able to make a major contribution to a publication such as this one (see, e.g., Tye 1990). What distinguishes the particular authors of this book is a commitment to a set of assumptions about global education. Two of these have been discussed already: (1) the individual school as the optimal unit for change efforts and (2) the importance of local teacher and school action for lasting school improvement. In addition, these authors, in general, accept the following definition of global education (which parallels the definition developed by Hanvey 1976):

> Global education involves learning about those problems and issues that cut across national boundaries, and about the interconnectedness of systems—ecological, cultural, economic, political, and technological. Global education involves perspective taking—seeing things through the eyes and minds of others—and it means the realization that while individuals and groups may view life differently, they also have common needs and wants.

Finally, the authors agree that global education is a social movement and, as such, calls for changes in schooling that promote the attitudes, knowledge, and skills encompassed in the preceding definition. We are not concerned with adding a unit or course on international affairs to the already overburdened curriculum. Neither do we wish to confine global education to social studies. Rather, global education calls for the infusion of a global perspective into *all* curriculum areas.

Context and Practice

This yearbook is divided into two sections. The first part examines the context of schooling in which a global perspective can and should be developed, and the second part is directed more toward issues of practice.

In Chapter 1, Lee Anderson develops a powerful rationale for global studies. First, he describes the convergence of three fundamental changes in the world's social structure: the growth of global interdependence, the erosion of western dominance, and the decline of American power and influence—both economic and political—in the past 20 years. Then he discusses the international influence on economic and political life in the United States over the past two decades, and he shows how our demography and culture are becoming more global in nature. Finally, he points to the link between social change and educational change and argues for global education as an accurate mirror of the direction in which society is moving.

Whereas Chapter 1 abounds with factual material for the thoughtful educator who wishes to develop an argument for a global education program in the schools, Barbara Tye, in Chapter 2, clearly delineates the problems inherent in changing the curriculum of a local school when complex issues like global education are involved. She views such change through a framework that separates the "deep structure" (the common characteristics supported by society) of schooling from the "unique personality" of each school. In so doing, she warns that globalizing a school's curriculum really is a "deep structure" change. Educators interested in changing must be aware of the many related effects of such a change—for example, reorganization of instructional patterns, relations with the community and the superordinate system, and collaboration across disciplines.

Rounding out this first section, Chapter 3, by Steven Lamy, sets forth a useful framework for gaining an understanding of current right-wing attacks on global education. Lamy shows how such attacks are wrongheaded, given today's interdependent world; and he suggests elements for a training program to help teachers involve students in global issues—while avoiding behaviors that so often are fodder for ultraconservative critics.

In the second part of this book, James Becker (Chapter 4) links global education to what is currently thought of as citizenship education. He reviews current offerings in the social studies and notes that the dominant structure of the field was set in 1916 and hardly prepares students for life in today's interdependent and complex world. He reviews current state-level curriculum reforms, with particular attention to the inclusion of global studies in history, economics, geography, and interdisciplinary courses. He points to the fact that true reform will come about when teachers are given the time to reflect and plan together.

In Chapter 5, Jane Boston discusses educational leadership in global education. She points out that educational leaders must have a clear vision of the role of the school in today's changing world, as well as the requisite skills needed to share that vision and encourage people to work toward it. She illustrates the relationship between global education and school leadership by discussing the behavior of individual principals and teacher leaders. Much of what she has to share is rooted in the literature on school change and her own extensive experience as a principal and as a consultant change agent. She demonstrates how global education can be a vehicle for educational leaders to bring about many of the related curriculum and instruction improvements that have been seen as desirable for many years.

In Chapter 6, Ida Urso examines the role of teachers in today's complex world, including the fact that they are faced with an ever expanding curriculum and a society that is less than grateful for what they do. Using qualitative data from the CHI study, Urso shows how global education can be a renewing force for teachers.

In Chapter 7, Jan Tucker explores the knotty problem of creating educational collaborations between schools and universities. In particular, he examines the qualities of successful global education partnerships, which have the following characteristics:

- an interdisciplinary nature,
- a focus on teacher development rather than on "teacher-proof" curriculums,
- an emphasis on local planning,
- an inherent ethical quality, and
- a mutually challenging and rewarding nature.

Tucker also suggests two major benefits from such global education: (1) the linking of preservice and inservice training efforts for teachers and (2) a natural tendency of such projects to focus in a healthy way on local multicultural issues. Finally, Tucker discusses the need and value of beginning such cooperative efforts with a search for commonly held definitions, goals, and conceptualizations.

In Chapter 8, Charlotte Anderson documents many ways in which global education involves schools and students with their communities. Further, she looks at such programs as Columbus in the World and the Network Project of CHI and shows how they (1) facilitate curriculum decision making, (2) promote and enrich interdisciplinary resources that might otherwise go untapped, and (3) stimulate community support. In this process, Charlotte Anderson enumerates and describes instructional materials and ideas that link the community and classroom in a search for better understanding of global issues.

In Chapter 9, Toni Fuss Kirkwood uses her experiences in Dade County, Florida, to show why and how global education has become a successful vehicle for school improvement. She looks at the impact of global education on curriculum, school organization and culture, administrative behavior, and teaching and student learning; and she provides guidance to efforts to train teachers to "infuse" a global perspective into their teaching.

Finally, in the Conclusion, I explore themes that emerged from the data gathered in the CHI study, such as (1) global education as a social movement, (2) the search for meaning in global education, and (3) competing demands in schooling and the effect on global education. These themes suggest many issues, such as membership in the movement, the sociopolitical context, definition, the problem of time, the press for accountability, teacher isolation, and the need for appropriate research strategies that involve practitioners. The exploration of these themes and issues ties together many of the ideas presented in previous chapters and suggests a possible agenda for future action on the part of those interested in global education and, more generally, school renewal.

Issues as Imperatives

Those of us who have participated in the preparation of this book believe it is an important piece of work. Obviously, we think that our ideas are correct and deserve to be considered. There are other, more critical reasons for believing it is important, however.

It has already been pointed out that citizens of today's world, more than ever before, need to learn attitudes and behaviors that recognize and promote interdependence and cooperation. The book begins with this idea, Lee Anderson's chapter thoroughly documents the realities, and every author reinforces this theme in his or her own way. Getting this thought understood by educators and concerned lay people is critical and is the main reason we believe this book is important.

As Steve Lamy points out in Chapter 3, there are those who do not wish to acknowledge the realities of today's world, who prefer to maintain the status quo because they are in positions of control or advantage. The status quo cannot be maintained, however; and efforts to do so can only jeopardize the well being of future generations.

As with any significant social movement, issues are neither simple nor straightforward. For example, a current strategy employed by some opponents of global education is to call for "balance" in the curriculum. Presenting a variety of views on a given subject, of course, is good education; and global educators should always see that this is done. What is ultimately important, however, is the analysis of varied positions and the motives of those who advocate them. Unfortunately, today's advocates of balance do not call for such analyses. Rather, they argue their positions and attack global education on ideological grounds. Global educators who seek always to include in the curriculum the positions of left- or right-wing critics, for example, without careful analysis of those positions, do a disservice to students. This approach constitutes propaganda, not education; and it is not a matter of balance.

We believe the *1991 ASCD Yearbook* is important because education leaders need to understand global education and the issues it encompasses. We believe that ASCD is the primary organization serving education leaders in America and, in fact, education leaders throughout the world. The people who will receive this book are, as Jane Boston describes in Chapter 5, exactly the ones who can and do make a difference. We hope *Global Education: From Thought to Action* clarifies for them what global education is, why it is important, how to bring it about, and how it can be used as a vehicle for the improvement of schooling.

References

Alger, C.F. (1974). *Your City in the World/The World in Your City: Discover the International Activities and Foreign Policies of People, Groups, and Organizations in Your Community.* Columbus: Mershon Center, The Ohio State University.

Bellah, R.N., R. Madsen, W.M. Sullivan, A. Swidler, and S.M. Tipton. (1985). *Habits of the Heart: Individualism and Commitment in America Life.* Berkeley: University of California Press.

Blumer, H. (1969). *Symbolic Interaction: Perspective and Method.* Englewood Cliffs, N.J.: Prentice-Hall.

Glaser, B.G., and A. Strauss. (1967). *The Discovery of Grounded Theory: Strategies for Qualitative Research.* Chicago: Aldine Publishing Co.

Hanvey, R. (1976). *An Attainable Global Perspective.* Denver, Colo.: Center for Teaching International Relations.

Tye, B.B., and K.A. Tye. (in press). *Global Education: A Study of School Change.* Albany: State University of New York Press.

Tye, K.A., ed. (1990). *Global Education: School-Based Strategies.* Orange, Calif.: Interdependence Press.

Part I

Context

1

A Rationale for Global Education

Lee F. Anderson

In the past two decades, a growing number of educators, government officials, business people, and civic and religious leaders have become involved in an education reform movement that at the precollegiate level is commonly called global education or international education. At the collegiate level, it is usually referred to as global studies or international studies.

The people involved in global education are trying to globalize American education in a variety of ways. Some of the movement's participants focus on expanding and improving the study of world history, world geography, world economics, world politics, or world ecology. Others seek to expand students' understanding of cultural diversity through the cross-cultural study of literature, art, music, dance, religion, and social customs. Many seek to expand and improve the study of foreign languages, including rarely studied languages that are of growing importance to the United States, such as Japanese, Chinese, Russian, and Arabic. Many global educators devote their energies to improving instruction about often-slighted regions of the world: Asia, Africa, the Middle East, and Latin America. Still others focus on improving education about world problems such as the maintenance of national security, the control of warfare, the reduction of world poverty, the promotion of human rights, and the preservation of ecological well-being.

Some global educators seek to place the study of American society and its history in a world context so as to highlight the ways in which American cities, states, and the nation as a whole are linked to the rest of the world. Some are teachers of teachers and thus focus on expanding the international education of teachers through undergraduate courses, inservice programs, and organized foreign travel. Some educators have created high schools that focus on international studies, and many colleges and universities have established international studies majors and programs that include studies abroad. Some global educators are particularly interested in devising ways to better use community resources in teaching about world affairs—for example, local people engaged in international business, Peace Corps returnees, foreign students, and individuals who actively participate in the international activities of local religious, community, or ethnic groups.

All these activities—and more—make up global education. To globalize American education is to expand opportunities to learn about the world beyond the borders of the United States, and to learn about American society's relationship to and place in the larger world system. Finally, it means helping American students to see things from the perspective of other peoples of the world.

This chapter sets forth a rationale for global education that consists of a three-fold argument: (1) that in the past two decades three basic historical changes in the social structure of the world have converged; (2) that because of this conjuncture of historical trends, American society became more globalized in the 1970s and 1980s and will likely become even more so in the 1990s and beyond; and (3) that education mirrors society in the sense that social change generates educational change. These arguments create a strong rationale for efforts to globalize American education.

Changing Social Structure of the World

In the past two decades, we have been experiencing a fateful convergence of three profound historical changes in the world's social structure that began at different periods of time. The first change, which has been under way for the past half millennium, is the accelerating growth of global interdependence. The second, which dates to the first decades of the 20th century, is the erosion of Western Civilization's dominance of the rest of the world. The third change, which dates from the early 1970s, is the decline of American hegemony in the world political economy.

Accelerating Growth of Global Interdependence

The growth of global interdependence can be seen in the expansion of technological, political, cultural, economic, and ecological networks connecting different peoples, cultures, civilizations, and regions.

Interdependence has been growing throughout much of world history. Only in the modern era (c. post-1400), however, has the scale of interdependence become worldwide. In the past five centuries, global interdependence has been a product of three interrelated events that have dominated and shaped so much of modern world history: (1) European expansion, (2) the emergence and growth of capitalism, and (3) the diffusion of modern science and technology. The growing global interdependence generated by this trilogy is clearly evidenced when we look at the world from a variety of disciplines.

History. The era in which human history was in large measure a collection of relatively isolated regional histories has ended, and an era of global history has begun. For example, it would be impossible to write a good history of modern Detroit without integrating it with a global history of the world automotive industry.

Geography. The isolating effects of distance have been reduced by the evolution of global systems of transportation and communication through which flow an ever-expanding traffic of people, money, information, ideas, goods and services, technology, diseases, and weapons. For example, think of the rapidity with which the stock market crash on Wall Street in October 1987 spread to the stock exchanges of Sydney, Hong Kong, Tokyo, London, Paris, and Frankfurt, or of the rapidity with which the AIDS virus is spreading across the globe, or of the ease with which we telephone family, friends, or associates on the other side of the globe.

Economics. The world's once largely separated local, national, and regional economies have been progressively incorporated into a single global economy. World markets have developed for virtually every element of economic life—consumer goods, technology, capital, minerals, energy, and labor. A rapidly growing portion of humankind has become dependent as both workers and consumers on these world markets. Hot summers in the American Midwest translate into higher bread prices in consumer markets across the world. Expanding steel production in Latin America, East Asia, and Europe translate into contracting labor markets in Pittsburgh and Gary. Under the auspices of a growing number of multinational corporations (MNCs), production has become highly internationalized. For example, the Ford Escort that is produced in Europe is assembled from component parts manufactured in 15 different countries. The volume of international trade and foreign investment has been expanding for several centuries, as has foreign lending and borrowing by governments. International organizations have developed that make and shape trade, monetary, and credit policy at the global level, for example, the General Agreement on Tariffs and Trade (GATT), the International Monetary Fund (IMF), and the World Bank.

Politics. The international political system has become progressively more integrated over time. Channels of communication interlinking governments have expanded. For example, more than 400 international organizations have developed over the past 150 years, and international conferences have become commonplace. The number of nonstate actors in world politics has grown dramatically, to include MNCs, terrorist groups, religious organizations, and individual citizens. Boundaries separating domestic and foreign affairs have been eroding; as a consequence, many social problems have become internationalized, including the control of drug traffic and other crimes, the maintenance of environmental health, and the management of inflation.

Sociology. An expanding array of social activities have become transnational in scope, including science, medicine, sports, tourism, entertainment, and education. Private transnational associations (associations with memberships in several countries), such as Rotary, the Salvation Army, Boy and Girl Scouts, and Amnesty International, have proliferated. The transnational activities of locally based organizations have radically expanded, for example, international relief work of religious and other groups, high school student-exchange programs, university programs involving studies in other countries, and the import and export activities of locally based business firms.

Demography. A planet that five centuries ago was characterized by a high degree of racial, religious, linguistic, and ethnic segregation has been substantially desegregated by the massive intercontinental migrations that have taken place in the past few centuries. Many countries are now ethnically and culturally pluralistic societies whose citizens are linked to many other parts of the world by virtue of race, ethnicity, language, religion, or cultural tradition.

Ecology. The Earth of the 20th century is a much more integrated planet than it was in 1400. The massive two-way exchanges of plants, animals, and microorganisms between the "Old" and "New" Worlds that followed European and African intrusion into the Americas, and European entry into Australia, New Zealand, and other Pacific islands, have substantially homogenized the plants and animals we eat as food. Viruses originating in the Eastern Hemisphere make us ill almost as frequently as the Western Hemisphere's home-grown varieties. Concerns over the depletion of the ozone layer, global warming, ocean pollution, acid rain, deforestation and desertification, toxic and nuclear waste disposal, and the extinction of animal and plant species are resulting in international cooperation.

Culture. The past half millennium has witnessed a marked homogenization of human culture. A global culture is developing. The technical language of this emerging culture is English. Its common ideology is science. Its characteristic social institutions are large-scale, globe-spanning, public and private bureaucracies. Its commonly shared technologies are jet planes, communication satellites, telexes, networks of interconnected computers, facsimile machines, and transworld telephone systems. But the historically recent growth of a global culture has not eradicated the rich array of distinctive regional, national, local, ethnic, and religious cultures, many of which predate the emergence of a global culture and others that have developed in response to it. To the contrary, the world's global microculture and its myriad distinctive microcultures coexist in a set of uneasy, often tense, and constantly shifting relationships.

Barring global nuclear war or a worldwide ecological disaster, there is no reason to anticipate that the centuries-long growth of global interdependence will end soon or even slow down. The historical record indicates that the growth of global interdependence has been accelerating throughout the modern era, particularly in this century, and likely will continue to do so. Were we able to quantify global interdependence and measure its growth as economists measure the growth of gross world product, we would undoubtedly see the statistician's familiar J curve produced by the logic of exponential growth. We would see global interdependence developing slowly between the 15th and 18th centuries, then a bit more rapidly in the 19th, and then dramatically in the 20th century.

Erosion of Western Dominance

As we all learned in our world history courses, Europe, in the early modern era, began to expand its geographical zone of control and influence. In 1400, Europe was only one civilization among many—and a comparatively underdeveloped one at that. By 1900, Europe, together with its former and existing colonies, extended its influence over 85 percent of the Earth's land surface.

But even at the height of western dominance, the beginning of the end was in sight. "The problem of the twentieth century," wrote the African-American leader, W.E.B. DuBois, in 1900, "is the problem of the color line—the relation of darker to lighter races of men in Asia and Africa, in the Americas and in the islands of the sea" (quoted in Stavrianos 1971). DuBois' prophecy has turned out to be remarkably accurate. In no small measure, the history of the 20th century is a story of increasingly successful resistance to western dominance. Rupert Emerson, an eminent scholar of colonization and decolonization, made a similar point: "A great era of human history has come to a close. . . the era of western dominance of the rest of the world" (Emerson 1960, 5). Emerson's observation is in error, but only because his verb tense was wrong. The era of western dominance has not ended, but it is clearly receding.

Western dominance has eroded in several ways. Its most dramatic political manifestation is the decolonization of the world, particularly since World War II. Within a very few decades, most 19th-century colonial empires were dismantled to be replaced by more than 100 newly established politically independent states.

The erosion of western dominance is manifest culturally in the renaissance and self-assertion of many very old cultures and religions long dormant beneath an overlay of western dominance. Perhaps, for Americans, the Islamic renaissance and the revival of interest in precolonial African cultures are the most visible examples. But they are only two among many.

The decline of western economic dominance is evidenced in several ways. Two of these are particularly visible to Americans. One was the emergence of OPEC and the two "oil shocks" of the 1970s that signaled the loss of direct western control over much of the world's petroleum industry.

The second probably has even more long-term consequences for the world as a whole and certainly for the United States. This is the relative decline in economic importance of the Atlantic Basin in the global economy and the relative increase in the importance of the Pacific Basin, a largely nonwestern part of the world. In the 1980s, the Pacific Basin became the world's fastest growing trading region. The Pacific is the home of the four most rapidly developing newly industrialized countries (NICs): South Korea, Taiwan, Singapore, and Hong Kong, as well as the home of five nations with very rich natural resources—Indonesia, the Philippines, Malaysia, Thailand, and Australia. Japan is the world's foremost supplier of capital, and China is by far the world's largest developing country with growing economic ties to the rest of the world.

Decline of American Hegemony

Hegemony exists in the world political economy when one country is simultaneously predominant in world agro-industrial production, in world commerce, and in world finance. As a consequence of its economic preeminence, that country enjoys an unrivaled degree of political power, military might, and cultural influence (Wallerstein 1984).

Periods of hegemony are historically rare and short lived. There have been only three instances of the rise and decline of hegemony in modern history. The first occurred in the mid-1600s when the United Provinces (the Netherlands) became a hegemonic power. Dutch hegemony lasted for about 50 years and then declined. The second instance occurred in the mid-1800s. In 1815, the United Kingdom emerged from the Napoleonic wars as a hegemonic power. The era of Pax Britannica lasted until the early 1870s, after which British hegemony began to fade.

The third instance centers on the United States. The United States began its ascent to hegemony in the late 19th century. About 60 years later, the United States emerged from World War II as the world's clearly hegemonic state. In the first 25 postwar years, the United States dominated world production, commerce, and finance; and the nation exercised an unequaled degree of political and cultural influence over the rest of the world. The era of undisputed American hegemony was short lived. In the early 1970s, U.S. hegemony began to decline.

There was a decline in productive preeminence. In the 1950s, with only 6 percent of the world's population, American factories, mines, and farms produced about 40 percent of the gross world product. By 1980, the U.S. share had dropped by almost one half to 22 percent (Gilpin 1987, 344). In the 1950s and 1960s, Detroit was the auto capital of the world; the United States produced about 75 percent of the world's automobiles. Today it produces about one quarter. In the 1960s American expenditure on research and development (R&D) was 50 percent more than that in the seven leading industrialized countries. Currently, as a percentage of its gross national product (GNP), Japan spends over 40 percent more on civilian R&D than does the United States, and West Germany spends over 30 percent more. In the first 25 years of the postwar period, most of the world's multinational corporations (MNCs) were American-based firms. Since then, the number of MNCs based in Europe, East Asia, and the Third World has been growing rapidly, and the relative U.S. share is declining.

As the United States' productive preeminence declined, so did America's commercial predominance, since the two are linked. The U.S. share of total world trade has been declining over the past two decades. In the first 20 years of the post-war period, U.S. firms produced 30 percent of world manufacturing exports. By the middle of the 1980s, the percentage had dropped to 13 percent. This figure points to the single most dramatic and significant manifestation of declining commercial preeminence, the growth of trade deficits. Since 1893, the United States had a merchandise trade surplus in every year until the 1970s. (That is, the value of exports exceeded the value of imports.)

The United States has not had a trade surplus since 1975. To the contrary, the deficit has steadily grown from a few billion dollars per year in the 1970s to about 171 billion a year in the late 1980s.

At the height of American hegemony in the 1950s and 1960s, the relative competitiveness of U.S. firms was such that many firms could out-compete foreign firms in the American domestic market. U.S. firms also could out-compete foreign firms in international markets, often in their competitors' home markets. Since the end of the 1960s, many American firms have been losing their relative competitive edge on both the domestic and international fronts, and hence the trade deficit.

Finally, the financial preeminence of the United States is waning. Within a very short time the United States moved from being the world's largest creditor nation to being the world's largest debtor nation. Being in debt to the rest of the world is not a new experience for the United States, of course. Economist Benjamin Friedman notes: "Like any newly developing country, America began its economic life as a borrower. Debts owed by Americans to foreign lenders probably started to accumulate as soon as the first permanent European settlers stepped ashore at Saint Augustine in 1565" (Friedman 1988, 223). At the time of independence, Americans owed about $70 million to foreign investors. By the time of the Civil War, net foreign debt was about $400 million.

Immediately after the Civil War, the United States invested heavily in railroads and steel production. A significant fraction came from foreign investors. By the 1890s, the American economy was sufficiently developed so that the need for foreign capital declined. Friedman notes that the "net international debt peaked at $3.3 billion in 1896" (Friedman 1988, 226-227). It took only two decades to eliminate 1896's $3.3 billion foreign debt. In 1915, the

United States became a creditor nation and continued to be for about 60 years. Indeed, the United States replaced Britain as the world's largest creditor nation.

In 1982, American foreign indebtedness began to increase rapidly. Early in 1985, we officially returned to what we had been throughout most of American history—a net debtor country. The foreign debt continued to grow after 1985. In 1987 our net foreign debt was about $400 billion, by far the largest of any country in the world, and has continued to grow.

Two points about hegemony bear restating: Historically, periods of hegemony are both rare and short lived. Hegemony is an abnormal state of affairs in the world political economy. At least up to this point in modern history, the emergence of a hegemonic state has been immediately preceded by a large-scale, highly destructive war: the Thirty Years War (1618-1648) in the case of Dutch hegemony, the Napoleonic Wars (1792-1815) in the case of British hegemony, and World War II in the American case.

World War II left America's enemies in ruin and many of our allies in shambles. The American people experienced the tragic death and maiming of many thousands of men and women, but the United States ended the war with its physical plant, infrastructure, and economy intact. Indeed, the war pulled us out of depression; moreover, wartime demand stimulated the growth of productivity in the nation's factories, farms, mines, and offices.

Thus, when the United States is compared with Europe, China, Japan and other parts of the world in 1945, there is no mystery regarding why it was able to assume a hegemonic position in the quarter century following the war. Nor is there much mystery associated with the decline of the nation's international predominance. With the U.S.-assisted recovery of Europe and Japan in the two decades after 1945, a *relative decline* in the global economic and political position of the United States was inevitable. What is mysterious in retrospect is why most of us who lived through the era of American hegemony came to look on U.S. preeminence as a natural state of affairs that would last forever. Few of us in the 1950s and 1960s could see these two decades to be what in fact they were—an abnormal and brief moment in the history of the world political economy.

Note that I used the term *relative* in speaking of declining American hegemony. What we have been experiencing in the 1970s and 1980s is not an *absolute decline* in American economic status, but rather a relative decline. To speak of declining hegemony does not mean that the United States is doing very poorly while other nations are doing very well. Rather, other nations are catching up with the United States, which, like a racehorse, bolted from the starting gate in 1945 and was furlongs ahead before other horses had begun to run.

Globalization of American Society

I now turn to the second link in my argument on behalf of global education. The recent convergence of growing global interdependence, eroding western dominance, and declining U.S. hegemony has substantially accelerated a broad process of social change that I am calling the globalization of American society. I am referring here to the growth of a network of two-way linkages that connect American society and the rest of the world.

Defined this way, the globalization of American society obviously is neither new nor recent. Quite to the contrary, the process has been underway at least since October 12, 1492. However, this long-term process has been rapidly accelerating over the past 20 years, in four areas of American life: the economy, politics, demography, and culture.

Globalization of the American Economy

The economic dimension of social life is a network of relations linking the production, exchange, and consumption of goods and services. In recent years, the economic life of the American people has become more globalized in many ways.

Imports and Exports. A growing fraction of goods and services Americans produce is exported, and a growing fraction of what Americans consume is imported. At the height of U.S. hegemony in the 1950s and 1960s, the American economy was at once globally preeminent and virtually self-sufficient. Most of the goods and services Americans consumed were produced within the United States. The dollar value of exports and imports combined was less than 10 percent of U.S. GNP in 1955. By the late 1980s, international trade accounted for almost 30 percent of GNP. Currently, more than one-fifth of U.S. industrial output is exported. One in six workers in manufacturing produce goods for export. The products grown on two of every five acres of American farmland are exported. More than 50 percent, or 24, of the 42 most important industrial raw materials are imported (Fred Bergsten 1983, 3-4).

U.S. Firms Abroad. Historically some U.S. firms produced for the domestic market, some produced for export to foreign markets, and some firms did both. But all of the firms had one thing in common: until recently, production took place almost exclusively within the national boundaries of the United States. This is no longer true. Today, a growing fraction of the production, assets, employees, and earnings of American firms is located outside of the United States.

As a consequence of recent technological innovations in world transportation and communication, coupled with the social logic of capitalism, a new type of business firm has rapidly developed, an enterprise commonly called multinational corporations (MNCs). Simply defined, an MNC is a firm with central headquarters in one country and production units in two or more countries. These production units can be factories, mines, farms, or service enterprises, such as hotels, restaurants, banks, insurance companies, and advertising agencies.

Today, most of the largest American firms, as well as many smaller ones, are MNCs engaged in internationalized production. One product or component thereof is manufactured in one country, another product or component in a second country, another in a third country, and so on. A sizable fraction of the assets and employees of American MNCs are located outside the United States. For example, 40 percent of Ford's assets and 58 percent of its employees are outside the United States. Proctor and Gamble has 19 percent of its assets abroad and 33 percent of its employees. Thirty-six percent of Coca-Cola's assets are in foreign affiliates, and over 50 percent of its labor force. A large share of many MNCs' revenues and profits derive from the sale of products produced by their foreign affiliates. For instance, in 1986, the output from the overseas factories of National Cash Register (NCR) accounted for 60 percent of the company's $6 billion of revenues. This output included computers made in Germany, automatic teller machines produced in Scotland, and computerized cash registers made in Japan. NCR's revenue dependence on sales made by its foreign affiliates is not atypical of American corporations. For instance, about 75 percent of Coca-Cola's operating income comes from overseas.

Manufacturing is not the only sector of the American economy that is becoming progressively more internationalized. Service industries are following on the heels of manufacturing with "global offices" supplementing "global factories." Bank of America has more than 250 foreign affiliates, the majority of which are in developing countries; Citicorp has more than 230. Holiday Inn operates over 100 foreign affiliates, many of which are in developing countries—as are most of Sheraton Hotel's foreign affiliates. The service sector's links to developing countries, indeed, reflect the increasing globalization of the markets of the industrial firms serviced by banks, hotels, and advertising agencies.

One multinational service industry is very close to home for most of us. McDonald's and Kentucky Fried Chicken are two of the nation's transnational fast food industries. The world's largest Kentucky Fried Chicken outlet (with 500 seats) is located in Beijing, and purportedly the world's busiest McDonald's is on the Ginza in Tokyo.

Before the mid-1900s, a few firms operated internationally; for example, Singer Sewing Machines produced in England for the British market at the turn of the century, and in 1911 Henry Ford had assembly lines in Europe. Only in the post-World War II period, however, have MNCs come into their own, after jet planes, container shipping, computers, and reliable transcontinental telephone systems became operational technologies in the evolving systems of global transport and communication.

A major surge of American direct foreign investment began in the 1970s. In 1965, American firms' foreign investment in physical assets amounted to about $45 billion. In 1970, this had grown to $75 billion; by 1975, to $124 billion; and in 1980, to $213 billion (Harrison and Bluestone 1988, 217).

Why the 1970s? The decline of U.S. hegemony provides a significant part of the answer. As noted previously, after the 1960s American firms faced increasing international competition. The consequence was a profit squeeze. Between the period of 1963-1968 and 1969-1975, net pre-tax profit rates fell dramatically in many industries.

Faced with this situation, corporate managers and their boards did what all good business people must do. They searched for strategies by which to halt the decline in profits and reverse the trend. One of the most popular strategies was to "go global" by shifting production out of the United States to acquired or newly constructed production facilities in other parts of the world. Some firms followed this path to enhance their market share in foreign markets protected by tariffs, quotas, or other restrictive trade practices. Other firms followed the strategy to reduce production costs by locating their operations in relatively low wage areas in the world economy or in places with a favorable business climate created by low taxes, minimal environmental protection regulation, favorable government subsidies, and so forth.

Foreign-Owned U.S. Firms. A growing share of the goods and services Americans consume are produced by foreign-owned American firms. On the day I wrote this part of the chapter, I consumed or used the following products: Pillsbury flour, Hills Brothers coffee, Carnation creamer, Friskies cat food and Alpo dog food, a Bic pen, Vaseline Intensive Care Lotion, Foster Grant sunglasses, a Burger King Whopper, Häagen-Dazs ice cream, Green Giant beans, Keebler cookies, Michelin tires, Shell gasoline, and a Seagram's gin martini. What do all these products have in common? It is the same thing that the following American firms have in common: Peoples Drugs, A&P, Ramada Inn, Bloomingdales, Brooks Brothers, Firestone, Doubleday, Viking Press, CBS Records, and 20th Century Fox. All the American products were produced by foreign-owned American firms, and all the firms are foreign-owned American businesses. For example, the Whopper, the Green Giant beans, and the Häagen Dazs ice cream are Pillsbury products; this firm is owned by Grand Metropolitan, a British multinational firm. A&P is German owned; CBS Records, Japanese owned; and 20th Century Fox, Australian owned.

Foreign investment in the United States is the flip side of American foreign investment abroad and, as previously noted, has been a part of the American heritage since colonial times. But while foreign investment in the United States has a long history, that history has been changing in several significant ways.

To begin with, the magnitude of foreign investment and its rate of growth in recent years are historically unprecedented. Most experts on the matter estimate that foreign investment in the United States now amounts to more than $1.5 trillion. This is a substantial increase from $196 billion in 1974 (Tolchin and Tolchin 1988, 6).

Second, direct foreign investment in real estate, land, and business firms has augmented portfolio investment, which was almost the sole form of foreign investment until recently.

Third, foreign investors are now putting their money into virtually every sector of the American economy. In the financial sector, foreign investors have increased their holdings of U.S. bank assets from $32 billion in 1973 to $445 billion in 1986. In 1973, 61 U.S. banks were more than 50 percent foreign owned, representing 22 countries. By 1983, there were 230 foreign-owned banks representing 53 countries; collectively, these banks controlled about 16 percent of total U.S. banking assets. A third of California's bank assets are foreign owned, and foreign-owned banks make some 40 percent of business loans in New York (Tolchin and Tolchin 1988, 7, 132, 316).

Foreign investment in the industrial sector of the economy has been growing, as well. Foreign investors have spent at least $200-300 billion in factories, warehouses, and assembly plants. Japanese investment in automobile plants is the most publicly visible. In addition to Japanese firms, European, Canadian, and Australian firms have sizable investments in manufacturing facilities. The Pennsylvania Department of Commerce (1989) recently reported that more than 140 foreign-owned manufacturing firms operated in the state, including 36 West German firms, 24 British, 16 Canadian, 6 Swedish, 6 Belgium, 5 Swiss, and 1 or more Irish, Spanish, French, and Australian firms, in addition to 13 Japanese firms. Nationally, 7.5 of every 100 American workers in manufacturing are employed by foreign-owned firms (Stokes 1987, 2334).

Real estate is yet another sector of the American economy in which foreign investment is rapidly growing. Estimates of the total value of foreign investment in U.S. real estate vary. The Department of Commerce's 1987 estimate is $24.5 billion, while other estimates exceed $100 billion. But even using the conservative figure, the rate of growth in foreign investment in U.S. real estate is striking, increasing from $799 million in 1976 to $24.5 billion in 1987, about a 3,000 percent increase in the last decade (Stolpestad 1989, 5, 7).

Fourth, not only has foreign investment in the United States been growing in volume and spreading across different sectors of the economy, it is coming from more places in the world than it once did. From the colonial era to the recent past, the origin of almost all of foreign investment in the United States was Europe (including Britain). Today, the lion's share of foreign investment continues to come from Europe, but Europe no longer has a monopoly. As of the mid-1980s, the top 10 investors, in ranked order from largest to smallest, were Britain, the Netherlands, Japan, Canada, West Germany, Switzerland, France, Kuwait, Australia, and Sweden.

There are several reasons that foreign investors with a great deal of money find the United States a good place to spend it. The nation is politically stable; it has the world's largest internal market; and since the mid-1980s, the value of the American dollar has declined in world currency markets, making many investments in the United States a good bargain. Firms, banks, and investment houses in Japan, Europe, and elsewhere have so much money to spend because of the U.S. trade deficit. American business firms and consumers are spending much more on imports than they are earning on exports. Imports are paid for in dollars, and since the value of imports exceeds exports, billions of dollars accumulate in the corporate treasuries and banks of the nations that export to the United States. These dollars, in turn, can be used to invest in the United States.

Pacific Basin Commerce. A growing share of the goods and services Americans produce and consume are consumed and produced in the Pacific Basin. For the past several centuries the center of gravity in the world economy has been located in the Atlantic Basin. Quite naturally, throughout most of American history, our primary economic relationships with the rest of the world centered on Western Europe; on West Africa; and, in the 19th century, increasingly on Latin America. Asia and, more broadly, the Pacific Basin were not ignored; but in the grand scheme of things, Asia and the Pacific were sideshows until the middle part of this century.

In the past half century, the Pacific Basin has become an increasingly visible and salient region in America's international environment; first militarily and then economically. Of the four major wars the United States has fought in the 20th century, two and one half were fought in the Pacific Basin. More young Americans have given their lives on the land, in the sea, and in the air west of Los Angeles than on battlefields east of New York. Moreover, it was in the Pacific Basin that the nuclear age began in August 1945.

U.S. trade with Pacific countries now exceeds in volume and value American/European trade. For every jumbo jet that traverses the Atlantic between the United States and Europe, four jumbo jets cross the Pacific between the United States and countries on the Pacific Rim. Four of the world's most rapidly developing NICs—South Korea, Taiwan, Singapore, and Hong Kong—account for a growing fraction of American trade, as well as U.S. foreign investment. The huge Chinese economy is growing. Much of the world's textile industry is located in China. Until June 1989, a growing number of American exporters were searching out Chinese markets, and an increasing number of American firms were investing in production facilities in China. It is likely that American/Chinese economic relationships will grow again sometime in the 1990s.

Then, of course, there is Japan, which is never out of our consciousness. No nation in the world gets more attention in America's business press. The reason is not hard to find. The United States and Japan have two of the largest national economies in the world; and, regarding trade, production, and finance, the two are among the world's most interdependent domestic economies. Indeed, they have become so integrated that the Japanese are purported to have invented a word for it: *Nichibei*. The word is a combination of Japanese characters for Japan, "Nibon," and characters for America, "Beikoku," meaning "rice country" (Gilpin 1987, 6).

The growing importance of the Pacific Basin in America's economic life does not mean that the nation's long-established relationships with Europe, Latin America, Africa, and Canada are losing their importance. The significance of trade with Western Europe, Latin America, and Africa is also rising: witness the maneuvering of American-based MNCs to be firmly in place in Europe when in 1992 the European Community (EC) becomes the world's single largest market with a population of 320 million. With the changes of the late 1980s in Eastern Europe and the Soviet Union, American economic involvement in this region is rapidly expanding. Finally, the world debt crisis in Latin America and Africa affects American banks and, through them, the entire American economy.

Foreign Borrowing. An increasing fraction of the goods and services Americans consume are financed through foreign borrowing. In recent years, maintaining the American standard of living has become increasingly dependent on borrowing from abroad. Robert Lawrence (1988, 32), a Brookings Institution economist, notes:

> In a closed economy, domestic production alone provides the resources for domestic spending. Living standards will thus depend only on the growth of factor inputs and the efficiency with which they are used to produce goods and services. In an open economy, however, other factors can affect living standards.

One of these factors is foreign borrowing, through which current levels of consumption can exceed current levels of production.

This is precisely what has been happening over the past decade—as suggested previously in the discussion of the U.S. international debt. In the first 25 years after World War II, American per capita spending increased annually at the rate of 2.2 percent, and most Americans experienced an increasing standard of living in the 1950s and 1960s. Since 1979, the growth of per capita spending (1.6 percent) has substantially exceeded the growth of per capita production (1.2 percent; Lawrence 1988, 33). The difference has been financed by a large increase in overseas borrowing. Foreign borrowing finances the trade deficit. In addition to the trade deficit, the United States has been experiencing a long series of large federal budget deficits. These deficits are financed through the sale of various U.S. Treasury securities. A sizable and growing fraction of the federal debt is purchased by foreign investors. Total foreign holdings of marketable U.S. Treasury securities increased from about $40 billion in 1975 to over $200 billion by 1985 (Tolchin and Tolchin 1988, 322).

This view of the globalization of American economic life and the ways in which the U.S. and world economies have been merging is shared by two well-known economists, one a neoconservative and the other a liberal. Despite their ideological differences, the two view the contemporary status of the American economy in virtually identical ways. Jude Wanniski (1978, 19) writes:

> The world is not fragmented, but integrated, which means that every economic event that takes place someplace in the world is felt virtually everywhere in the world. And theories that treat the U.S. economy as if it were closed when in fact is in constant interaction with the rest of the world are likely to be deficient or worse.

Robert Reich (1989, 23) writes:

> America itself is ceasing to exist as a system of production and exchange separate from the rest of the world. One can no more meaningfully speak of an "American economy" than of a "Delaware economy." We are becoming but a region—albeit still a relatively wealthy region—of a global economy, whose technologies, savings, and investments move effortlessly across borders.

Internationalization of American Political Life

Wanniski, the neoconservative, goes on to observe: "To the degree the world is economically integrated it is also politically integrated, because there is no divorcement of economic and political events" (Wanniski 1978, 20). Thus, it is not surprising that the accelerating globalization of the American economy is paralleled by an increasing internationalizing of American government and politics. American political life is becoming more internationalized in many ways; three are noted here.

States' International Involvement. State and municipal governments are increasingly involved in international economic policy. Conventionally, we think of foreign policy as the sole province of the federal government. But as Chadwick Alger (1977) has demonstrated, this conventional view is inaccurate and incomplete. Virtually all large groups and organizations, private as well as public, have foreign policies. State governments, for example, participate extensively in international economic affairs.

The National Governors' Association reported that 44 of the nation's governors traveled abroad one or more times in a recent year in search of export markets for the products of their states. Collectively, states spend substantially more on foreign investment promotion than does the federal government. As of 1987, 35 states maintained 84 offices abroad, and both numbers undoubtedly have increased since then ("Innocents Abroad" 1987).

Foreign Involvement. Foreign firms with large investments in the United States are becoming more involved in American politics. We are familiar with the direct and indirect involvement of American-based MNCs in the politics of other nations. We have also been experiencing the converse of this tradition. As Bruce Stokes writes: "Foreign investors are emerging as major new players in the American political process. This development is a logical and inevitable outgrowth of America's insatiable demand for foreign funds in recent years" (Stokes 1987, 2333).

Many foreign firms retain lobbyists in Washington, D.C. In addition, many American affiliates of foreign-owned companies maintain Political Action Committees (PACs) that are active in American election campaigns. Political influence is virtually impossible to measure with any precision or apart from specific instances of its exercise, but most observers agree that as foreign investment in the United States grows, so does the political influence of the investors. As Stokes (1987, 2333) observes:

> To protect their mounting stake in the American economy, foreign investors, just like U.S. business executives, are becoming more involved in U.S. politics. And elected officials increasingly are responding to their needs because foreign investment means jobs for constituents and economic growth back home.

Loss of Economic Sovereignty. Researchers for the Hudson Institute, a major "think tank" for the American business community, have observed that, "as the world economy has become more integrated, the United States, like all other nations, has progressively lost control of its economic destiny. . . . Although economic integration has been underway for many years, its impact has only become decisive in the U.S. within the last two decades" (Hudson Institute 1987, 3).

Lester Thurow, Dean of the Massachusetts Institute of Technology's management school, dramatizes the general point: "You could argue that [Federal Reserve Chairman Alan] Greenspan has an obsolete job. He's supposed to control the American money supply" (*Chicago Tribune*, April 23, 1989, 22). One of Greenspan's associates, Keith Johnson, would undoubtedly agree:

> After largely having its way in the world economy for decades, the U.S. is now involved in a global give-and-take. For the first time in this century, foreign investors have the power to profoundly influence the pace of American economic activity. Accommodating this new reality will be a major challenge for Washington's policy makers in the next few years (Johnson, July 6, 1987, 36).

Continuing Cosmopolitanization of the American People

More than a century ago, Walt Whitman wrote, "America is a race of races." Today, the long-term cosmopolitanization of American demography is being accelerated. In the very apt term of Joel Kotkin and Yoriko Kishimoto, the United States is becoming a "world nation, with ethnic ties to virtually every race and region on the planet" (Kotkin and Kishimoto 1988, 2). They note that Hispanics and Asians now constitute nearly 10 percent of the population and are the fastest growing groups in the society. Non-European Americans (i.e., Asian and Pacific Americans, Native Americans, and African Americans), combined, will make up one-third or more of the population by the year 2000 and probably more than a majority by the end of the next century (Kotkin and Kishimoto, 168).

In many cities and some states, non-European Americans will constitute a majority of the population well before the year 2100. In California, a majority of the state's elementary and secondary students are of Hispanic, Asian, and African origin (*New York Times*, April 12, 1989, 16). Los Angeles is often referred to as the second largest Spanish-speaking city in the Western Hemisphere, and I have heard Miamians describe their city as the southern-most Anglo city, the northern-most Hispanic city, and the western-most African city.

Just as economic affairs and political life in the United States are becoming progressively more globalized, so are American people themselves. We are becoming a world nation within a world system.

American Culture and the Growth of Global Consciousness

To no one's surprise, as American economics, politics, and demography become more globalized, so do many sectors of American culture. Popular or mass culture is clearly one of these. As noted previously, hegemony consists of not only economic predominance but of unequaled cultural influence as well. In the era of American hegemony, however, Norman Cousins wrote of the widespread diffusion of American popular culture:

> A new musical comedy erupts into success on broadway and within a matter of weeks its tunes are heard all the way from London to Johannesburg, as though they had pre-existed and were waiting only for a signal from the United States to spring to life. Or a new movie about the Russia of a half-century ago will be made from a book, and all over the world the theme song from *Doctor Zhivago* will be a request favorite of orchestras. . . .

> Few things are more startling to Americans abroad than to see youngsters affect the same unconventionalities in dress and manner, whether in Stockholm, Singapore, or Sydney. The young girls with their flashing thighs on Carnaby Street in London or on the Ginza in Tokyo; the young males with their long hair and turtleneck sweaters (with or without beads) in Greenwich Village or the Left Bank or Amsterdam or Hong Kong—all seem to have been fashioned by the same stylists of alienation and assertion (Cousins 1968, 20).

Today many elements of mass American culture continue to be exported to the rest of the world: witness the continuing worldwide popularity of

American movies, TV shows, soft drinks, and fast foods. But with eroding western dominance and declining American hegemony in a world of growing global interdependence, American popular culture, in turn, is influenced by the rest of the world. Popular music provides a good example. Gone is the era when American parents could surprise and impress their adolescent children by demonstrating familiarity with Anglo-American rock music. *Newsweek* recently told me what I had intuitively guessed from occasionally listening to music enjoyed by my own children and by the college students I teach. "From Bulgaria to Boston, Zaire to Martinique and New York to Paris, pop is going global. As never before, exotic imports and weird new hybrids are flourishing: African reggae, Moroccan flamenco, even Cambodian heavy metal" (Miller, 1988, 72).

The movie industry shows similar trends toward a global culture. In a recent *New York Times* article entitled "Hollywood Takes to the Global Stage," Charles Slocum, an analyst for the Writers Guild of America/West, observes: "The foreign markets interest American producers, and the U.S. markets interest foreign companies. What you end up with is companies in all countries looking outside their borders" (Stevenson 1989, 1). As Hollywood becomes more dependent on revenues from the international distribution of American films, producers make creative decisions about such matters as plots and casting with an eye toward movie audiences outside the United States. The cosmopolitanization of American popular culture is but one facet of a broad and powerful cultural change in several sectors of American society. Americans are developing a cognitive awareness and comprehension of the global unity, or interconnectedness, of many dimensions of the world.

For example, many scientists and their popularizers emphasize the unitary nature of the Earth's natural system. A 1988 cover story in *U.S. News and World Report* notes: "Scientists are finding a depth of complexity and interconnections among the Earth's systems unimagined even a decade ago. Air, water, rock—and life—affect and depend upon one another" ("Planet Earth" 1988, 57).

The social sciences are undergoing a similar kind of intellectual shift. When the modern social science disciplines emerged in the 19th and early 20th centuries, most economists, political scientists, anthropologists, and sociologists depicted the social structure of the world to be a collection of separated, independent, and autonomously developing societies. Today, many scholars see the social world to be a singular, complex, albeit still little-understood, global system. Eric Wolf, a prominent anthropologist, says, "the world of humankind constitutes a manifold, a totality of interconnected processes" (Wolf 1987, 3).

Area studies (e.g., African studies, Soviet studies, and Latin American studies) illustrate the emergence of a global consciousness in social science scholarship. Kenneth Prewitt, writing as president of the Social Science Research Council, notes:

> Area scholars are liberating themselves from the now exhausted debate over their relationship with traditional disciplines. . . . This frees area studies to take up a new and much more consequential challenge. To repeat the obvious: horizontal interdependencies being what they are, it won't do to study China as if there were no Latin America [or] as if there were no Africa. To this cliche, we add another: vertical linkages being what they are, it won't do to study global energy consumption, international violence, or world hunger and population pressure as if those things did not start in and return to haunt the many households and villages where people work and worship, play and procreate. Some part of what area studies will be about in the next decade is connecting the local with the international, the village with the world system (Prewitt 1982, 2).

Because so much of "America's business is big business," as one American President once observed, changes in the culture of the business community undoubtedly influence U.S. society far more than do intellectual changes in the social sciences or even in the physical and life sciences. In the American business community, a dramatic explosion of global consciousness has occurred. Long gone are the days when talk about things global was scorned as an exercise in "global baloney." Terms like *global* or *global perspective* may be seen as alien, dangerous, or un-American within some parts of the American educational community; but within the prevailing culture of American business, *global* and its various derivatives, such as *globalization* and *globalized*, are terms with prominent places in the lingua franca of industry, commerce, and finance. One cannot read business publications—such as *Business Week*, *Fortune*, and *The Wall Street Journal*; the business sections of major newspapers; or the trade journals in many industries—without encountering the term *global* dozens of times.

Global consciousness has also grown in the philanthropic side of the American business community. Small American foundations are following in the steps of large foundations, such as Ford, Rockefeller, Carnegie, and Kellogg, in focusing on global concerns. The Council on Foundations reported an increase in foundation spending on global projects from $96 million in 1983 to $227 million in 1986. Such an increase reflects a growing concern about global environmental issues and an awareness that national borders are no barriers to the spread of illegal drugs, or AIDS, or the movement of refugees and the spread of terrorism. Reflecting on the 1989 annual meeting of the Council on Foundations, the president of the Rockefeller Foundation, Peter Goldmark, observed: "There are people here from Arkansas, Wisconsin and Georgia, and what they are hearing and saying is that 'global issues' and 'local issues' are becoming the same issues" (Teltsch 1989, 7).

Social Change and Educational Change

Not only have there been vast changes in the social structure of the world and an increasingly global orientation in American society, but educational institutions are evolving to accommodate these changes. (See Chapter 2 by Barbara Tye for a more extensive discussion of educational change.)

Educational institutions and processes are not isolated from the economics, politics, demography, and culture of society. On the contrary, as historians and sociologists of education are fond of reminding the rest of us, education mirrors society. The primary motors driving educational change are located outside the educational system, in the society at large. Thus, social changes generate educational change, albeit not by any simple formula of linear translation or through an automatic, conflict-free, and resistance-proof process in which educators play only passive roles.

Examples of the linkage between social change and educational change abound. For example, think of the relationship between the coming of the factory system and the growth of universal primary education in the early 19th century. Recall the link between the growth of large-scale corporate and public bureaucracies in the late 19th and early 20th centuries and the expansion of secondary education. Look at the numerous ways in which American education has been influenced by the civil rights and feminist movements. Ponder the impact, direct and indirect, that the development of television has had on children and young people's schooling.

*   *   *

My case on behalf of global education is grounded in three related propositions:

1. In the past two decades, three historically profound and mutually reinforcing changes in the world's social structure have converged: Global interdependence is rapidly increasing while western dominance is eroding and American hegemony is declining.

2. The convergence of these changes is globalizing many facets of American society, including its economy, polity, demography, and culture.

3. Education mirrors society in the sense that social change generates educational change.

The argument for global education constitutes a rationale that does three things. First, it provides a plausible explanation of the past. As a reform movement, global education emerged in the 1970s and grew in visibility and influence in the 1980s. The movement has experienced both failure and success, but on the whole education has become more globalized in the past two decades. This is what we would expect to observe if, as I have argued,

American society has become substantially more globalized in the 1970s and 1980s, and education mirrors society.

Second, the rationale provides a reasoned forecast of the future of global education. We can anticipate that American education will become even more globalized in the 1990s and beyond because it is likely that American society will become even more globalized in the near future. The three historical trends that have globalized American society are likely to continue into the future because they are self-reinforcing.

Third, the rationale provides an intellectually sound and socially responsible justification for globalizing American education. To ask why American education should be globalized is analytically comparable to asking why American driver education should be "right laneized." There is no intrinsic or inherent value in teaching new drivers to drive in the right lane of two-lane roads because right-lane driving is not intrinsically superior to left-lane driving, as our British and Australian friends will attest. But once it became a historical fact that America is a right-laned society, rather than a left-laned one, then the undisputed responsibility of driver education was to develop within American drivers the particular set of motor, perceptual, and cognitive skills associated with right-lane driving.

In an analogous sense, there is no inherent merit in a globalized education compared with a nationalized or localized education. This is the case because there is no intrinsic value in being an increasingly globalized society within an increasingly globalized world. What if Americans belonged to an increasingly independent and isolated society in a world of other increasingly independent and isolated societies? Would such a society be "better" or "worse"? Rather than try to answer this question, let us face the historical reality of interdependence.

Young American citizens inherit a society that is becoming progressively more involved in and dependent on a world that simultaneously is becoming more interdependent, less dominated by one of many historic civilizations, and less subject to U.S. control. Given this historically determined fact, we have no choice but to press on with the task of globalizing American education. To do otherwise would be intellectually stupid and socially irresponsible because we would be putting at risk the children we love, the students we teach, and the nation we cherish.

References

Alger, C. (June 1977). "'Foreign' Policies of U.S. Public." *International Studies Quarterly.*

Bergsten. F. (1983). *The United States in the World Economy.* Lexington, Mass.: Lexington Books.

Cousins, N. (July 1968). "Needed: A New World Theme Song." *Saturday Review.*

Emerson, R. (1960). *From Empire to Nation.* Boston: Beacon Press.

Friedman, B. (1988). *Day of Reckoning*. New York: Random House.

Gilpin, R. (1987). *The Political Economy of International Relations*. Princeton: Princeton University Press.

Harrison, E., and B. Bluestone. (1988). *The Great U-Turn: Corporate Restructuring and the Polarization of America*. New York: Basic Books.

Hudson Institute. (1987) *Workforce 2000*. Indianapolis, Ind.: Hudson Institute.

"Innocents Abroad." (November 23, 1987). *Fortune*.

Johnson, K. (July 6, 1987). "The Growing Foreign Policy Role in U.S. Policy. *Fortune*.

Kotkin, J., and Y. Kishimoto. (1988). *Third Century: America's Resurgence in an Asian Era*. New York: Crown Publishers.

Lawrence, R. (1988). "The International Dimension." In *American Living Standards: Threats and Challenges*, edited by R.E. Litan, et al., Washington, D.C.: The Brookings Institution.

Miller, J. (June 13, 1988). "Pop Takes a Global Spin." *Newsweek*, pp. 72-73.

Pennsylvania Department of Commerce (1989). *A Sample Listing of U.S. Affiliates of Foreign Companies in Pennsylvania*. Harrisburg, Pa.: Pennsylvania Department of Commerce.

"Planet Earth: How It Works and How to Fix It." (October 31, 1988). *U.S. News and World Report*.

Prewitt, K. (1982). *Annual Report*. New York: Social Science Research Council.

Reich, R.B. (May 1, 1989). "As the World Turns." *The New Republic*.

Stavrianos, L.S. (1971). *The World Since 1500: A Global History*. Englewood Cliffs, N.J.: Prentice-Hall.

Stevenson, R.W. (April 16, 1989). "Hollywood Takes to the Global Stage." *New York Times, Business Section*.

Stokes, B. (September 19, 1987). "Foreign Owners." *National Journal*.

Stolpestad, J.A. (1989). "Foreign Investment in U.S. Real Estate." Senior honors thesis, Department of Political Science, Northwestern University: Evanston, IL.

Teltsch, K. (April 19, 1989). "Small American Foundations Focusing on Global Concerns." *New York Times*.

Tolchin, M., and S. Tolchin (1988). *Buying Into America*. New York: Times Books.

Wallerstein, I. (1984). *The Politics of the World Economy*. New York: Cambridge University Press.

Wanniski, J. (1978). *The Way the World Works*. New York: Simon and Schuster.

Wolf, E. (1987). *Europe and the People Without History*. Berkeley: University of California Press.

2

Schooling in America Today: Potential for Global Studies

Barbara Benham Tye

One of the persistent paradoxes of the educational enterprise in America is that any individual school is very much like other schools, yet at the same time also uniquely itself. This paradox can be explained by the existence of a "deep structure," which is determined by the basic values and assumptions that are widely shared throughout a society. This structure shapes the educational system of that society in its most fundamental aspects (B. Tye 1987) and affects the success of changes that may occur, such as the inclusion of global education.

Structure of Schooling

In discussions of change in school curriculums, organization, or management, educators often use the terms *top-down* and *bottom-up* to describe decisions imposed from administrators or boards versus decisions made by teachers, students, and parents. The different levels of school administration, instruction, and participation compose what people usually refer to as the school structure. In this chapter, however, I propose a more inclusive, three-level model of school structure: First, undergirding us all, is the society we live in; second, built on that society, is the set of cultural and social norms and assumptions concerning educational systems (the "deep structure"); third, supported by the first two levels, is the individual school.

Societal Perceptions

The nature of the deep structure of schooling is such that it could not change independently of a significant and prior change in the society as a whole. Indeed, we are talking about society's overall worldview when we talk of the deep structure of schooling. For example, when Western Civilization regarded children more or less as little animals in need of taming, schoolmasters treated children accordingly. Much more recently, as our society, for a variety of reasons, draws more and more women of child-rearing age into full-time employment outside the home, the custodial (i.e., babysitting) role of schools has taken on increasing importance. A major shift in societal perception about what schools are for has occurred in the 20th century: We now expect schools to solve a myriad of social problems. Some of these problems did not even exist in earlier times; others were considered by most Americans to be the proper responsibility of the family, the church, or other social institutions.

Deep Structure

We can recognize the deep structure of schooling by identifying and examining those aspects of public education we all tend to take for granted: *But of course* the school building should consist of rooms of about that size. But of course the curriculum should consist of separate subjects, taught as if they had little or no relationship to each other. But of course the school day should be divided into six or eight approximately equal chunks of time. And by no means should children have any significant choice about what, when, or how they will learn, or about the rules they should live by while at school. These are only a few of what Sarason (1982) refers to as "regularities" of schooling that are seldom questioned; other assumptions concern the norms of the teaching profession, the role of parents and community members in the daily life of schools, and the hierarchical nature of the educational bureaucracy. These are the characteristics of schooling now, at the close of the 20th century, that are assumed to be right and thus are seldom seriously questioned. That's what everybody expects schools to be like; that's the deep structure of schooling.

It is important to remember this pervasive, shared aspect of the deep structure. Each school does not have its own deep structure; the deep structure of American schooling (or of any other country) is nationwide. It is this connectedness that gives the deep structure its persistence and its power. The deep structure changes very seldom, and only when the society at large is already leading the way.

Unique Personality of Each School

Built on the foundation of the deep structure is the unique personality of each individual school. At this level, no two schools are exactly alike. Each school is shaped by its own history, by the nature of the community of which it is a part, and by internal factors such as the quality of teacher/administrator relationships, the number and intensity of school problems, and the climate of most of its classrooms. At this level, it doesn't matter that schools from Maine to California are using the same textbooks, dividing up time (schedules) and space (classrooms) in the same way, treating teachers similarly, and approaching discipline problems in almost identical fashion. Setting the deep structure aside, one can still walk into a school and get a feel for its individuality. Spend a week there and you may—if you have asked the right questions—know enough about the place to identify the primary components of that school's unique personality.

We can generalize about schools when discussing elements of the deep structure, but we must be very careful about generalizations when discussing a particular school. Assumptions we carry with us into a school setting may not hold up, or they may blind us to the actual realities of that particular school. For example, a dark and gloomy inner-city school that looks like a factory from the outside may, despite scarce resources and other problems, be a happy place inside. Leadership could be superb, faculty morale could be high, students could feel cared for and productive. Likewise, a beautiful new school in the suburbs could feel quite flat and lifeless inside. We cannot really know a school's personality until we have spent some time there, studying it—or even living it.

Aspects of a school's personality can change, sometimes quite rapidly. The most obvious source of change would be the assignment of a new principal, but there are many others—staff turnover, loss of extra funding, changing community demographics, and public recognition that the school is doing a good job. Even something so seemingly mundane as new furniture and a coat of paint in the teachers' lounge can contribute to a change in the way that school feels to the adults who spend their working days there.

Changes in the personality of a school can also be deliberate—planned and carried out by administration and staff as part of a school improvement effort. Improving staff interaction, solving specific school problems, building mechanisms for shared decision making, and other goals for school improvement at this level are extremely worthwhile. They can go a long way toward making an individual school a happier and more productive place.

We have seen that the deep structure of schooling is inseparable from a society's most fundamental assumptions about what schools are for. It tends to resist any attempts to change it, unless such attempts are in tune with changes also occurring in the society as a whole. The personality of each school, on the other hand, is receptive to change efforts that are planned and responsive to changes that are unplanned. It is always in the process of adjustment, as it assimilates such changes and, like an organism (and it is a social organism), struggles to maintain its equilibrium (see Figure 1).

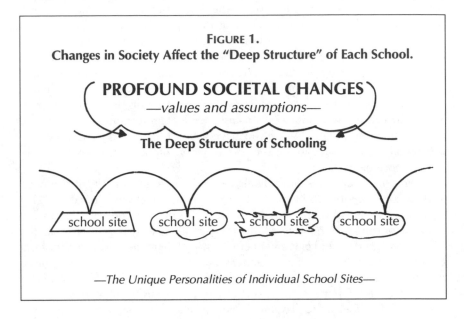

FIGURE 1.
Changes in Society Affect the "Deep Structure" of Each School.

PROFOUND SOCIETAL CHANGES
—values and assumptions—

The Deep Structure of Schooling

school site   school site   school site   school site

—The Unique Personalities of Individual School Sites—

Direction of Educational Change

Given the characteristics of society as a whole, the deep structure of schooling, and the unique personality of individual schools, the direction of lasting educational change becomes clear: significant and long-lasting change flows from the society to the deep structure, and finally from the deep structure into the individual school. Such change is often (though not necessarily) officially sanctioned by legislative mandates, court rulings, and policy making by state and district boards of education. It is crucial to recognize, however, that major educational change cannot be legislated or mandated if it is not in tune with a concurrent shift in overall public values and assumptions; it will simply wither away. School people can get cynical because they see so many policies and programs come and go over the years. "That was the big thing when I first went into teaching, and here it is again!" "We tried that 15 years ago, and it didn't work *then*." Any seasoned educator can think of many examples of sound educational practices that didn't catch on because they ran counter to the prevailing deep structure of the time.

Might it be possible for change to flow the other way, from the individual school into the deep structure? Possible, perhaps, but extremely improbable. My guess is that even if every elementary and secondary school in the nation were to abandon homogeneous ability grouping (for example), that would not be sufficient impetus to change our society's deeply ingrained belief in hierarchies of merit and ability. More than likely, pressured by their communities, schools would drift back into ability grouping within a few years. School-based decision making is another idea that comes around at regular intervals but always fades away again, victim to our society's faith in top-down management.

My basic premise is that we are in a time of transition, when a change in the direction of global awareness is taking place at the macro, societal level, as well as the micro level, in some individual schools and school districts. Between these two levels lies the deep structure of schooling, which is highly resistant to change. Only if my premise is correct—that we are in the midst of a "sea-change," moving toward a society that places more value on being globally literate—are we likely to see a similar shift in the deep structure of schooling.

Profound Societal Change

Some Historic Social Movements

Following Copernicus, Europeans had to get used to the strange idea that the earth was not, after all, the center of the universe. At about the same time, the voyages of discovery were proving that the earth was round. Heretical when first proposed, these ideas took about three generations to become an accepted part of the western worldview. "In the third and fourth generations," proposes E.F. Schumacher, "they have become the very tools and instruments through which the world is being experienced and interpreted" (Schumacher 1973, 90). Or, as Thomas Kuhn puts it, "when paradigms change, the world itself changes with them" (Kuhn 1970, 111).

Similarly, humans have not always thought in terms of being loyal to a nation-state. The concept of the nation-state did not exist in western thought before Charlemagne unified France. Twentieth-century minds, however, take the idea of national loyalty so much for granted that it is difficult to think of how the world could be anything other than the currently familiar configuration of sovereign nations. We make the mistake of assuming that because this is the way it is now, it must be the way it has always been. It comes as a surprise to learn how recent a pattern of social organization the nation-state actually is.

The idea of democracy—self-government by the common people—is also quite new, as is the related idea of individualism. Culture-bound as we are within the late 20th- century worldview, we find it almost impossible to understand the collective/communal mentality of medieval Europe (or, for that matter, of present-day cultures that are much more community oriented and far less individualistic than our own).

To understand the deep-structure phenomenon, one must be able to step back and see society as an historical process composed, in part, of social movements that arise, take hold for awhile, and eventually give way to new ones. These social movements are linked to what Schumacher (1973) calls the "great ideas." These concepts are born in controversy but, in time, become intrinsic, unquestioned, taken-for-granted components of a culture's worldview. Of course, this process does not happen in a vacuum. There must be something else going on within that culture for a great idea to capture the popular mind at a particular point in time.

Toward Global Awareness

Global awareness is a social movement in its early stages. As Lee Anderson pointed out in Chapter 1, since midcentury the powerful forces of economics and technology have been preparing us to think increasingly in terms of international causes and effects. A stock-market crash now is a worldwide disaster. Multinational corporations do business across national boundaries, with no allegiance to any one government. Electronic media enable people around the world to actually watch an event as it is happening. And perhaps more profoundly than we yet realize, the space-exploration program has enabled us to turn around and view our home planet from a distance so great that we can see how small it really is. We also must cope with the knowledge—also very recent—that mankind has the tools with which to destroy life on this planet totally in just a few hours. Indeed, the adjustments currently under way in the human psyche are just as mind boggling as those faced by the average European in the 1500s.

Profound societal change is always systemic, with effects rippling outward to touch our culture in its farthest corners. Like an ocean wave, though, it is often difficult—if not impossible—to pin down exactly when and where it begins. Like a wave, societal change gathers force and builds, swelling steadily to the point at which anyone would acknowledge its existence.

Now, nearing the end of the 20th century, we have come to feel that complexity and systemic interconnectedness are the natural order of things. Americans are slowly but steadily becoming more globally aware. American farmers and stock market analysts keep a close eye on the agricultural policies of the Soviet Union—drought in the Ukraine can mean money in the pocket for the Iowa wheat farmer. American consumers now know that there is no longer such a thing as an "American" car, and they are increasingly aware of the far-ranging effects of environmental problems caused by human activity, such as pollution of the oceans and destruction of the stratospheric ozone layer. Sometimes, as Lee Anderson points out in Chapter 1, global awareness comes in a rush: Witness the worldwide democracy movements in 1989—vanquished in China and victorious in Eastern Europe. Suddenly the breach in the Berlin

Wall awakened our interest in world events and gave us the sense of "living in history."

Systemic Responses to Change

In Chapter 3, Steve Lamy describes in depth the varied reactions to global education of groups with "contending worldviews." The systems that make up our society—economic, technological, political, cultural, and environmental—react to profound social change in different but predictable ways. I have already referred to the organismic attempt to maintain or regain equilibrium. In social terms, one might think of the reaction as an effort to defend and maintain the status quo. Powerful vested interests have a stake in preventing major change, unless they can see a way to make it work profitably for them.

Resistance can take many forms, including social violence, political campaigns, civil disobedience, and less noticeable kinds of simple noncompliance. Ordinary people find it hard to give up the comforts to which they have become accustomed—air conditioning, for example—even though they know that such a luxury contributes to an environmental problem that could prove disastrous for their own grandchildren. On an individual level, we find many ways to justify our own resistance to change.

The same is true at an institutional level. In the late middle ages the Catholic Church went through spasms of violent reaction to a social climate that was increasingly inclined to question long-accepted church doctrine. White American southerners, as a group, went through convulsions of negative reaction to the civil rights movement of the 1960s, though that movement was clearly part of a deep-structure change in American society, a change characterized by rededication to the democratic notion of social justice. In summary, then, one possible set of responses to profound social change is resistance—individual, group, and institutional—and all kinds of attempts to keep things as they were.

The other category of response involves adaptation to change. As the new worldview becomes increasingly acceptable—as the wave swells and gathers force—systems within a society adjust. Eventually a reconfiguration within or between social institutions may take place, along with the inevitable redistribution of power. For example, the growth of a large, merchant middle class in Europe in the late Middle Ages permanently changed the distribution of power of Western Civilization, undermining both the church and, eventually, the monarchy. The change currently taking place—to an increasingly global society—is producing many interesting reconfigurations. The increasingly transnational nature of economic institutions, for example, is teaching us to think in terms of a global economy rather than of separate national economies. These changes may eventually undermine national political systems in ways we cannot now foresee.

Resistance and adaptation are also evident in the American system of public education, as this vast institution confronts increasing national and international global awareness.

Adaptation and Resistance in Education

Adaptation at National and State Levels

Interestingly, the upper levels of the American educational bureaucracy seem to be responding positively to the growing global awareness of society. The business community and political groups such as the National Governors' Association (NGA) have encouraged educational involvement in global education. For example, the NGA 1988-89 Chairman's Agenda calls for international education and asks, "How can we as governors increase public awareness that the 'rules have changed,' and that we need a broader view of the culture, language, geography and history of other nations?" (p. 9). State departments of education across the United States are designing and implementing ways to incorporate global/international studies into the K-12 curriculum (see Chapter 4, by James Becker). In some states, such as Arkansas and California, the impetus comes from legislation; and the programs are supported by appropriations from the state treasury. In others, such as Florida, higher education has taken the lead; and programs are funded by private foundations. In many states, consortiums of like-minded organizations, such as World Affairs Councils, civic groups, and local colleges and universities, have joined forces with school districts to promote global education programs. During the past few years, the media have called public attention to the embarrassing performance of American elementary, secondary, and college students on basic tests of global knowledge. In response, influential organizations such as the National Geographic Society have put millions of dollars into international education projects for the public schools.

In 1987, a blue-ribbon commission, supported by a grant from the Rockefeller Foundation, published its final report calling for emphasis in four curricular areas:

- A better understanding of the world as a series of interrelated systems: physical, biological, economic, political, and informational-evaluative.
- More attention to the development of world civilizations as they relate to American history.
- Greater attention to the diversity of cultural patterns both around the world and within the United States.
- More training in policy analysis both of domestic and international issues (Study Commission on Global Education 1987).

Clark Kerr, who chaired the commission, concluded his preface to the report by saying, "We trust that this report will generate discussion at school, district, state board, and association levels, and that its central theme of education for United States citizenship in an interdependent world will serve as a guide for educators and policymakers."

At its March 1989 annual conference, the Association for Supervision and Curriculum Development (ASCD), one of the largest organizations of professional educators in the United States, passed 12 Resolutions for Education, one of which stated, in part:

> ASCD supports programs that present multiple perspectives and divergent points of view on international policy issues in order to encourage students to think critically, clearly, and independently (ASCD in press).

In the fall of 1989, ASCD established a Global/International Education Commission composed of designated members from each of the 50 states and six foreign countries. The purpose of the commission is to stimulate interest in global education at the state level.

There is more going on in support of global/international education at the national level than even the most knowledgeable global educators can keep track of: The wave is building. In part, it gets its power from the growing belief that a globally aware citizenry is in the national interest. More important, it also derives power from the increasingly pervasive understanding on the part of ordinary citizens that their own well being and that of their children is linked to the well being of people around the world and depends on international solutions to global problems.

Resistance at the Deep-Structure Level

Developments at the national level suggest that global awareness as a social movement is gaining momentum within our society, and may even be making some inroads into the deep structure of schooling. Whether it really will do so remains to be seen: we know how persistently the deep structure tends to resist change. One characteristic of American education is something that Jonathan Kozol once dubbed "nonstop forward motion"—our tendency to move from one educational goal to another and then to another, leaving earlier goals unmet (Kozol 1973, 6). This phenomenon can be viewed as a resistance mechanism. If it works as it usually does, we will see a flurry of global education activity at state and local levels over the next few years, and then it will fade away and some other focus will take its place. Thus would our educational system reject permanent change at the deep structure level.

The premise of this chapter, however, is that this time it will be different. This time we will see some lasting and significant deep-structure change, because society is changing, too. The next section addresses how individual schools might respond to these changes.

Global Awareness at Individual Schools

School-Based Change

At the school level, certain kinds of change are inevitable. They generally are responses to changing local or school-site conditions, and they may be changes for the better or for the worse. Other kinds of changes—often called school improvement efforts—can be planned and carried out by a determined faculty and staff, given support from the administration and district.

School-based change has strong support in the educational literature of the past 20 years (Bentzen 1974; Goodlad 1975, 1984; K. Tye and Novotney 1975). Nevertheless, the tension between centralized and decentralized decision making seems to be one of those never-ending and probably irreconcilable debates in the field of education. The evidence from research and practice indicates that decentralization has great potential for making schools happier and more productive work places for both adults and children. The deep structure of our educational system, however, favors centralization.

Interaction of Deep Structure and Individual Schools

Because of the influence of the prevailing deep structure, only certain kinds of school-specific changes have the potential for success. If a school faculty decided to tackle a change that was rooted in the deep structure of schooling, it would most likely fail, if the change ran counter to the deep structure. But suppose the deep structure is in a period of transition, as it now may be. Interesting possibilities exist for individual schools and districts during such a time. Some changes might be *regressive*, in that they attempt to recreate elements of past successes that were in tune with the waning deep structure. Or they could be *progressive*, "ahead of their time," as we say; such changes might be more in tune with the emerging patterns of societal belief and behavior.

We can already see these two extremes, as well as a range of intermediate responses, in individual schools across the country. Even within a single district, unique personalities of particular schools can be very different. One school may be moving full steam ahead to introduce global awareness into its curriculum, while not far away, another school will be focusing on other, more traditional goals, such as improving its reading programs or its test scores. (An irony often missed by people who know little about global awareness education is that an excellent reading program can easily incorporate elements of global awareness, and that test scores are actually likely to rise at the school that has global awareness as one of its themes.)

Resistance and adaptation, the major categories of response to social and institutional change, can also be found within and between schools as the pressure for global awareness intensifies at the societal level. The national educational reports, media attention, state legislation, and other national and state forces mentioned earlier are being noticed by the American public—and by American teachers. Local conditions, too, can increase teachers' awareness of global connections: for example, many teachers in some parts of the country "have the world in their classrooms." In schools with diverse student populations, cross-cultural awareness (an element of global awareness) and attention to mutual respect and understanding become essential parts of the curriculum.

School-Level Adaptations

Adaptation involves reconfiguration. When the principles of global education are applied in individual schools and school districts, certain reconfigurations seem to follow almost naturally. For example, global education lends itself to cooperative learning; indeed, I can hardly imagine how teachers could introduce global perspectives into their curriculums without using some forms of small-group work. This, then, is a change from the traditional "teacher talks/students listen" format so familiar to us all.

Another reconfiguration involves the return to a more interdisciplinary curriculum. Students in a science class studying the greenhouse effect use knowledge and skills from many disciplines: data collection (research skills); reading, letter writing, and composition (English or language arts); a study of geography and social and political implications (social studies); and even calculations of effects such as rising ocean levels or persistent drought conditions in "breadbasket" areas of the world (math). Students can even illustrate possible scenarios, or write and produce a play on the subject. None of the contemporary problems and issues that cut across national boundaries can be studied by using one discipline alone.

A third reconfiguration of the curriculum would be a change in the way the school relates to its immediate community. Teachers who work to incorporate some global awareness into their teaching tend to make greater use of community resources than has been customary during the past half century. Guest speakers, for example, become an important part of the learning experience. And projects such as *Columbus and the World*—in which the students themselves go out into their community to research the ways in which their city, town, or neighborhood is connected to other parts of the world—are a natural expression of global awareness education (Alger 1974).* In Chapter 8 of this book, Charlotte Anderson discusses how schools can productively interact with their communities as they pursue global studies.

These three changes—cooperative learning, interdisciplinary curriculum designs, and use of the community as a learning resource—are not new, and

---

*The curriculum for *Columbus and the World* was developed at Ohio State University and field tested in the Columbus, Ohio, public schools in the early 1970s. Since then, it has been replicated in many parts of the country with great success. For further information, contact the Mershon Center, Ohio State University, 199 W. 10th Avenue, Columbus, OH 43210-2399.

they certainly are not unique to global education. But these reconfigurations are more than simply compatible with global education; they are almost inevitable. I predict that more and more school districts will respond to the growing societal emphasis on global awareness by promoting these three adaptations. Indeed, many districts are already immersed in cooperative learning strategies.

School-Level Initiatives

A school that chooses global awareness as one of its central themes will find itself in exciting new territory. Its faculty might undertake many creative projects. For example, students and teachers together could carry out recycling projects to enhance environmental awareness, plan "international fairs" to celebrate the cultural diversity of the student body, or become involved in a telecommunications project with students in another country—communicating through a computer-and-satellite arrangement. Teachers will find that collaborating across disciplines to plan curriculums around global themes is a stimulating and professionally rewarding experience. Both Ida Urso in Chapter 6 and Toni Fuss Kirkwood in Chapter 9 describe teachers' positive experiences in global education projects.

School-Level Resistance

When it comes to implementation in an individual school, global education can be whatever a faculty wants it to be. No group of global educators could (or would) say, "This is what global education should look like in the classroom," pointing to one particular program. The open endedness of global/international education has great appeal for certain types of people, but others find it disquieting and tend to resist it.

Resistance at the individual-school, or micro, level takes several forms. Research on how people react to innovation shows several distinct types of reactions. "Innovators" are involved in designing the plan, and "early adopters" jump right in; but the "early majority" want to become familiar with the innovation first. Members of the "late majority" wait to see how it goes for the others before becoming involved; and a few people resist or reject the change altogether (Rogers 1962, 168-171). Implementation of global awareness education in the individual school must acknowledge and accommodate these disparate reactions—from both teachers and students.

Resistance at the individual school level can also come from any part of that school's unique personality. For example, when the relationship between a teaching staff and the principal is strained, the principal may find ways both obvious and subtle to stifle initiatives proposed by teachers. Conversely, teachers may refuse to become involved in projects that they know the principal supports. For global education to work, everyone must cooperate willingly and openly: it needs to be a schoolwide project.

The relationship between the school and the community it serves can also affect the school's success in introducing global education. If the parents and taxpayers harbor suspicion and distrust toward the school, success may well depend on the strategies chosen for implementation, the ways in which the community is informed about and involved with the efforts to globalize, and the school administrator's skill in public relations. As I mentioned earlier, however, closer ties with the community seem to be one natural component of global awareness education. Perhaps such an initiative on the part of a school could actually be the vehicle for improvement of school/community relations. In cases where the relationship is already a good one, efforts by school people to use their community as a learning resource are likely to be welcomed and appreciated.

* * *

As we approach the 21st century, it is possible to travel throughout the United States and find many schools involved with global awareness education. Sometimes the efforts are sponsored by the district, in which case one finds clusters of schools involved and collaborating. In other locations, only one school alone in a district, driven by the nature of its unique personality, might be working on building students' global awareness. From New York City to rural Arkansas to suburban Orange County, California; from Washington State to Florida—schools nationwide are responding to the profound societal shift currently underway in the world. My original premise seems to hold up: Increased global awareness occurs simultaneously at both the societal level and at the individual school level. Each reinforces the other. At the macro level, world events demand our attention and convince us of our need for global knowledge. At the micro level, more and more individual schools and school districts are beginning to include global awareness among their objectives for school improvement.

The deep structure of schooling, that intervening level which is both so slow to change and so powerful in shaping what happens in schools, is bound to be affected as more and more people—not only the larger community, but also teachers, administrators, parents, and students—learn to think globally as well as locally. It's an exciting time to be involved with schooling.

References

Alger, C. (1974). *Columbus and the World: A Curriculum*. Columbus, Ohio: Mershon Center, Ohio State University.

Association for Supervision and Curriculum Development. (in press). *Synthesis of Resolutions through 1990*. Alexandria, Va.: ASCD.

Bentzen, M.M. (1974). *The Magic Feather Principle*. New York: McGraw-Hill.

Goodlad, J.I. (1975). *The Dynamics of Educational Change*. New York: McGraw-Hill

Goodlad, J.I. (1984). *A Place Called School: Prospects for the Future*. New York: McGraw-Hill.

Kozol, J. (January 1973). "Moving On—To Nowhere." *Saturday Review/Education* 55: 6.

Kuhn, T.S. (1970). *The Structure of Scientific Revolutions*. Chicago: University of Chicago Press.

National Governors' Association. (1989). *America in Transition: The International Frontier.* Washington, D.C.: National Governor's Association.

Rogers, E. (1962). *Diffusion of Innovation*. Glencoe, Ill.: Free Press.

Sarason, S. (1982). *The Culture of the School and the Problem of Change*. Boston: Allyn and Bacon.

Schumacher, E.F. (1973). "The Greatest Resource—Education." In *Small Is Beautiful: Economics As If People Mattered*. New York: Harper and Row.

Study Commission on Global Education. (1987). *The United States Prepares for Its Future: Global Perspectives in Education*. New York: Global Perspectives in Education/The American Forum.

Tye, B.B. (December 1987). "The Deep Structure of Schooling." *Phi Delta Kappan* 69, 4: 281-284.

Tye, K.A., and J.M. Novotney. (1975). *Schools in Transition*. New York: McGraw-Hill.

3

Global Education: A Conflict of Images

Steven L. Lamy

*G*lobal education programs have been influenced by the criticisms of extremist ultraconservative interest groups in communities across the United States. In the past, this controversy may have arisen in the vacuum left by vague and ambiguous definitions of global education. I propose that the best way to avoid major controversy is to clearly define the substantive focus and the learning objectives of any interdisciplinary program. On the other hand, I believe it is impossible to avoid controversy when teaching international or global issues. Controversy is inevitable, and it should be welcomed by educators as essential to the learning process. The ultraconservatives seek to end this important aspect of critical thinking and propose that we introduce students to a "set of truths" that define the role of the United States in world affairs.

Differing images of global education are being promoted by formal and informal interest communities throughout the United States. If anything, the controversy over global education is shaped by contending images of how the world is and how it ought to be. The recent controversy is fueled, first, by an increasing frustration over the role of the United States in international affairs. Second, the controversy is shaped by debates about what role schools should play in the political education of students. Much of the global education controversy is accentuated by educators who often are more reformist oriented than are other groups in the community.

At the weekend conference sponsored by the Center for Human Interdependence (CHI) at Chapman College, during which this book was planned, I reviewed data from the CHI global education network project. My particular interest was in seeing what light those data shed on the issue of controversy over global education.

CHI offers K-12 educators a variety of educational services, from on-site curriculum assistance to institutes focusing on strategies for teaching about controversial issues. A review of program reports and teacher interviews suggests that the staff of CHI has not built its program around any specific definition of global education. Generally, CHI programs promote the development of a broad range of skills and competencies by offering participants interdisciplinary, substantive programs that also could be considered "transdisciplinary."

Interview data included notations by teachers and administrators that they were exposed to information and lesson plans in areas important to global education: self-awareness, cooperative learning, critical thinking, cultural understanding and empathy, and conflict resolution. In addition, CHI enhanced their skills in reading, writing, and information gathering.

The content of CHI programs does not reflect a traditional international relations agenda. Workshops, seminars, and institutes are primarily focused on the *human-centric* side of international affairs, with offerings such as future studies, folklore, cross-cultural awareness, human rights, comparative literature, basic human needs, and refugee issues. The *state-centric* issues of international affairs are not ignored: CHI has sponsored programs in international conflict, global political economy, ecological politics, and controversial issues.

Although many would argue that the focus on *human-centric* issues and the interdisciplinary nature of CHI's programs is suggestive of a reformist (i.e., change-oriented) agenda, there is no evidence to suggest that staff members or program consultants have made any effort to push a particular worldview or promote an agenda for radical change in American foreign policy. Only two speakers, outside consultants hired by CHI, were categorized by some participants as presenting a biased, anti-U.S. position. Interview data show that both speakers focused on very emotional and highly politicized issues. One speaker, who discussed international economic issues, was perceived by some participants as putting too much blame on the United States for the world's economic woes. As economic competition increases and the U.S. wealth, status, and decision-making authority in international economic affairs decrease in relation to Japan, Western Europe, and the newly industrializing countries of Asia, the frustrations associated with this relative loss of power are spreading throughout U.S. communities. This potentially volatile situation is accentuated in California by the tremendous increase in Asian migration and Asian investment. Frustrations often become the basis for racist and even xenophobic attitudes. In this situation, it appears that some program participants were looking for a more pro-U.S. description of relevant issues and corresponding neomercantilist economic policy prescriptions.

Several criticisms were also raised about a program that focused on U.S. foreign policy and refugees in Southeast Asia. Interviews with participants, as well as program evaluations, suggest that the instructor presented her views on the subject based on personal experience in refugee camps, but did not present any competing perspectives. Again, because of the proximity of teachers to issues (e.g., their classes are populated by Southeast Asian refugees) the chances for disagreement were significant. These sorts of disagreements are to be expected in any program that deals with public issues. There is always controversy over the allocation of goods, services, opportunities, and political decision-making authority; and both cases involve questions of distribution and redistribution of public goods.

CHI program staff were also caught up in the national debate about global education. Several school administrators asked about CHI's connections with the United Nations, which is still erroneously described as world government by polemicists. Several teachers and administrators asked if CHI were at all connected with "secular humanists and nuclear disarmament advocates" at the University of Denver. This comment is in reference to U.S. Department of Education study that critically reviewed curriculum materials developed by the Center for Teaching International Relations (CTIR) at the University of Denver.

Critics of Global Education

In his study, "Blowing the Whistle on Global Education," Gregg Cunningham (1986) conducted a personal review of the CTIR materials. He found them to be biased toward what he considered to be naive world order values such as peace, social justice, and economic equity. Using his own political view as a point of reference, he equated global education with globalism, liberalism, and utopianism. Furthermore, he accused CTIR staff and, by inference, other global educators of being ideologues guilty of misinterpreting reality and attempting to convert young students to their millennial cause:

> Social scientists often define politics as the process by which societies decide who gets what, when, where, how, and in what amounts. By that definition, every issue raised by any program of global education is a political issue—and often a political issue of the most controversial sort. This fact creates the possibility of academic abuse through undisclosed philosophical bias. Some globalists have, at least in a general sense, been quite candid in conceding the value-laden nature of their objectives. CTIR, for instance, boldly proclaims its quest for a "new world order" and dismisses those who resist the creation of this new age millennium as "miseducators" (p. 2).

Cunningham's report was promoted and widely distributed by a variety of ultraconservative organizations such as the Eagle Forum and the National

Council for Better Education. This report was circulated among California educators, and a few administrators within CHI schools were concerned with some of the charges. It is hard to ignore statements suggesting that global education ignores and at times misrepresents U.S. history, criticizes our government and its constitution, and seeks to denigrate patriotism (Schafly 1986).

Cunningham's report and the resulting reports, studies, and articles, however, represent the ideas of ultraconservatives or "movement conservatives" in American politics (Fitzgerald 1987). In domestic politics, such conservatives usually emphasize individual freedoms, a laissez-faire economic system, minimal government interference, and traditional religious and community values. Most movement conservatives have a passion for international relations and seek to carry their conservative social reform movement to foreign lands. They believe the United States is a redeemer state with a mission to take its values to the world, but they are pessimistic about the chances for world peace and equality. Most movement conservatives would embrace a Hobbesian view of international relations—conflict is endemic and self-help is the guiding precept for national leaders (Lamy 1988).

This Manichean view (i.e., good versus evil) of the world has a profound impact on the classroom. First, by accepting this more nationalistic view, one rejects a pluralistic assessment of world affairs. Pluralists reject the "my country right or wrong" assumption and recognize that at certain times American policymakers could be wrong and other states' leaders could be correct. For those on the political right, this position of "moral equivalence" is not acceptable. Global education, according to Phyllis Schafly (1986), promotes indoctrinating students with "the falsehood that other nations, governments, legal systems, cultures, and economic systems are essentially equivalent to us and entitled to equal respect." From Schafly's viewpoint, presenting students with the idea that systems are similar in many respects is naive and simply wrong. The social studies classroom, according to those who hold this view of the world, should prepare students to confront the enemies of American ideals. These ideals are defined as "Truths." Thus, global educators who encourage critical thinking and the "weighing of evidence" from contending perspectives are seen as guilty of imposing their social and political preferences on students, encouraging disrespect for American institutions and culture and rejecting the core assumption of the ultraconservatives: The American system is the best system and we have a mission to bring our ideals to the rest of the world.

It is not easy to respond to adherents of this worldview, especially when their patriotism and nationalism descend to chauvinism and dogmatism. Dogmatists on the left or right of the political spectrum are attracted by simple and permanent solutions. Their beliefs drive them to fanaticism and absolutes. No purpose is served by trying to reason with dogmatists or to urge them to consider other viewpoints. They are enemies of pluralism and pluralistic approaches and, thereby, will never be convinced that global education is of any value—unless it is defined in neomercantilist terms for the right or is promotive of socialistic visions of the future for the left. Unfortunately, these extremist voices tend to attract a great deal of public attention.

Goals of Global Education

When confronted by questions about "political objectives" of their programs and when asked to clarify the goals and objectives of global education, the CHI staff responded by referring critics to Robert Hanvey's *An Attainable Global Perspective* (1976). Hanvey's definition promotes five interdisciplinary dimensions of global education:

• *Perspective consciousness*: An awareness of and appreciation for other images of the world.

• *State of the planet awareness*: An in-depth understanding of global issues and events.

• *Cross-cultural awareness*: A general understanding of the defining characteristics of world cultures, with an emphasis on understanding similarities and differences.

• *Systemic awareness*: A familiarity with the nature of systems and an introduction to the complex international system in which state and non-state actors are linked in patterns of interdependence and dependence in a variety of issue areas.

• *Options for participation*: A review of strategies for participating in issue areas in local, national, and international settings.

This general definition of global education does not call for reshaping the world. The CHI staff believes that an education based on these intellectual dimensions will help prepare students to make informed choices in the future. Educators who were initially concerned about the political dimensions of global education seemed relieved when the CHI staff shared the Hanvey definition and discussed the more specific elements of their program. A few administrators were still apprehensive about the label "global education" and the implications of a stateless, interconnected, transnational community. These educators agreed to work with CHI if they could call it international, multicultural, or cross-cultural education.

It is clear that avoiding controversy is impossible, because of the different images of the international system. All interest groups want the schools to promote their image of the past, present, and future. However, the CHI strategy is to build its programs around a clearly stated definition of global education that emphasizes substance over value-laden mush. This strategy has proven effective in avoiding controversy. There may not be agreement with the conceptual priorities of a program, and some groups may be concerned about resources, speakers, and specific program topics; however, a program that

53

is shaped by an intellectually sophisticated conceptual definition is at least defensible. It is clear that programs will attract critical attention if they are developed to promote a specific vision of the future. Global education efforts must take unusual care to introduce teachers and students to *contending theories* that explain the actions of state and nonstate actors and describe the characteristics of human relations in the international system.

CHI-sponsored seminars and workshops were interdisciplinary in their focus and tended to be built around *human-centric*, substantive issues. In the language of traditional international relations, CHI programs favored low political issues such as the environment, human rights, and cultural affairs, over the high politics issues of international security. Their programs also encouraged participants to introduce students at all grade levels and in all subjects to concepts and issues that could be used to describe global realities. Lessons aimed at introducing students to concepts like interdependence, conflict, change, diversity, and economic well being were an essential part of their programs.

Because many of these concepts encourage a more pluralistic view of international relations, they are considered unacceptable by many individuals and groups more comfortable with a view that recognizes and promotes the U.S. as the hegemon or rulemaker. The point here is that no matter how careful educators are to provide multiple perspectives on an issue or problem, they will be criticized if they do not reinforce the view that the United States is the primary world leader and the sole representative of what is good in the international community. Global educators will always be in some trouble because the issues they teach and the skills of critical thinking and comparative inquiry that are so much a part of their programs challenge the assumptions of a state-centric system. State leaders are all taught that sovereignty should never be relinquished. Likewise, citizens are socialized to believe that maintaining sovereignty will require great sacrifices, including giving one's life for the cause. This is why we spend trillions of dollars on arms.

Is it any wonder that people are confused when our leaders start talking to traditional enemies and that teachers who encourage students to go beyond our "Cold War" perceptions of the Soviet Union are criticized by conservative interests? A warming of relations with an enemy or a shift in U.S. status in world affairs will begin to challenge individual assumptions or belief systems. It is this conflict between worldviews that is the primary cause of the global education controversy.

A final word about definitions of global education programs is appropriate here. Successful global education efforts that have worked around the unavoidable criticisms of dogmatic interests have generally structured their efforts around the following intellectual goals (Lamy 1987). These include:

• Global education programs should introduce participants to substantive and verifiable information that represents the findings of international scholarship in all disciplines. Furthermore, these studies should represent many cultural, historical, gender-related, and ideological perspectives.

• Courses or programs in global education should provide participants with opportunities to explore the core assumptions and values that define their worldview and compare it with worldviews held by individuals in communities across the international system. Programs should encourage participants to examine their images of the world as they evaluate critical international issues and prepare to respond to them.

• A global education program must prepare students for the future by introducing them to a wide range of analytical and evaluative skills. These skills will enhance students' abilities to understand and react to complex international and intercultural issues. For example, well-constructed global education programs should introduce students to the research process—an information-gathering process that involves the formulation of testable propositions and data gathering aimed at confirming or refuting these propositions.

• As Hanvey (1976) suggested in his conceptualization of global education, a defensible program in global education must introduce students to strategies for participation and involvement in local, national, and international affairs. Courses should provide relevant information that increases students' capacity to act or participate in public policy debates. Comprehensive global education efforts should emphasize the relationship between global issues and local concerns.

This brief discussion of conceptual frameworks serves to illustrate the importance of avoiding vague and ambiguous definitions of global education. While global education is by definition transdisciplinary, it is not everything for everyone. Many groups singled out for criticism have advanced normative assessments rather than empirical studies of controversial international issues. Although change might be possible and desirable, it should be the goal of every global education program to prepare students to critically assess information gathered across time and cultures and then formulate an agenda for policy action. Instructors in schools and colleges do teach values: It is impossible to present an entirely objective view of public issues. However, instructors should neither promote a specific policy agenda nor unfairly discourage students from conducting critical analyses of policy decisions.

The controversy surrounding the promotion of global education in U.S. schools is more than just a difference of opinion about how to teach and what should be taught. It is a dispute over images and the realities of power, authority, and agenda setting in both domestic and international politics. The participants in this dispute see the world quite differently. They disagree over the structure of the international system, the salience of issues, and the very language and values used to define the international system. This conflict is spilling over into the schools because individuals and interest groups do not agree on an agenda for civic education.

Contending Images of the International System and Global Education

This section explores some of the motivations behind the ultraconservative criticisms of global education. There are explanations for the controversy. The first proposition is that this controversy is fueled by increasing frustration among certain groups over the changing role of the United States in the world system described by Lee Anderson in Chapter 1 of this book. Such groups are reluctant to accept a relative decline of U.S. power and prestige, particularly in economic policy areas.

A second possible explanation relates to differences in worldviews. Simply stated, teachers and administrators who are active in global education programs generally have more "reformist" attitudes than educators who are not involved in such programs. These "reformists" represent a minority in the schools and in their communities. More troubling is that within many communities, the more ultraconservative voices, previously considered recessive positions, are gaining more influence in public affairs.

My goal here is not to defend or refute these propositions, but to encourage debate among educators and community leaders in an effort to discourage extremism and support reasonable and substantive discourse about how best to prepare students for the future.

There are at least four interest communities with contending worldviews who seek to influence and perhaps control global education programs in U.S. schools. The group with the most influence in U.S. communities has a neomercantilist, or national-interest, view of how schools should organize global education programs. This view corresponds with the dominant worldview in international politics: realism (Lamy 1987, 1988). Those who ascribe to this position believe that global education should prepare U.S. citizens for participation in an anarchic and competitive international system where self-interest rules and where chances for cooperation are limited. From this viewpoint, the prime mechanism for achieving a state's goals is through the threat or use of force. Furthermore, students should be prepared to represent U.S. interests in a Hobbesian world of conflict and competition. To neomercantilists, the world is divided between friends and foes; and our educational system should prepare students to compete and to secure our national interests. A unilateral approach is favored over all other policy options.

A second worldview, which is gaining increased support among educators, examines global issues from the perspective of an international society or community. This more reformist position recognizes both the need and potential for cooperation in attempting to respond to global problems and challenges. This is also a more pluralistic view of the international system. Power is defined in terms of a variety of attributes and not only military force. A state's position in the world is in part determined by its interests and expertise. This communitarian view of the world places a high value on cooperation, multilateralism, and burden sharing (Keohane and Nye 1989, Maghrooi and Ramberg 1982, Vasquez 1986). Thus, proponents of global education who hold this worldview would emphasize many of the educational goals suggested by Robert Hanvey and discussed earlier in this chapter. Dominant educational themes associated with this worldview include (a) recognizing the limits imposed by an interdependent political system, (b) exploring opportunities for cooperation, and (c) realizing that the community of states faces common crises that require a reassessment of self-help and highly competitive (i.e., winner-take-all) foreign policy orientations.

Though not dominant in our society, this communitarian worldview is a significant, if not majority, view among teachers and administrators who support global education in the schools. Herein lies a source of conflict. Those who do not support the more reformist vision, yet recognize the importance of some global education, generally support the national interest or neomercantilist view. For them, long-term or institutionalized cooperation means the loss of sovereignty; and the politics of accommodation is akin to appeasement.

Two minority, or recessive, worldviews are those of the utopian left and utopian right. The utopian left represents either Marxist or non-Marxist system transformers who seek to create a more equitable international system through the creation of socialist systems in which power is decentralized and economic well being, social justice, and peace are dominant domestic and foreign policy goals. Although the utopian right, or ultraconservatives, tend to label all global educators as proponents of this position, those interest groups who advocate this position do not play a significant role in the schools. More value-laden positions do not encourage a pluralistic approach (i.e., one with contending perspectives) to education.

The second recessive worldview is actually becoming more influential in educational debates. This is the ultraconservative, or utopian right, position discussed previously. Adherents of this view believe that the purpose of global education is to promote U.S. interest and to build domestic and international support for American ideals and traditions. We should be sharing our successes, our values, and traditions with the entire world. The ideal world, for ultraconservatives, is one shaped by American hegemony in economic, political, and cultural affairs. Those global educators promoting a more reformist line that emphasizes cooperation and power sharing are seen as misinformed, naive, and irrational. In a competitive system, failure to maintain power is a cardinal sin.

The conflict between the core assumptions of the communitarian worldview and the ultraconservative worldview is the primary source of the present global education controversy. Proponents of the former actually are not far away, ideologically, from the neomercantilists. In fact, the U.S. business community has strongly supported global education efforts aimed at increasing U.S. citizens' awareness of basic geography, foreign language, and world issues. Unfortunately, this healthy collaboration has been disrupted by reformists and utopians on the left, who criticize global educators for selling out to neomercantilists, and by the ultraconservatives, who claim global educators are delivering America to our enemies. The debate is unlikely to subside.

All of the factors that encouraged and emboldened the ultraconservatives are still prevalent. A major cause of concern for this group is the relative decline of U.S. power in the international system. In military terms, most believe that the Soviets are stronger than the Americans, and they quickly dismiss reforms in the Soviet Union as political maneuvers aimed at lulling the United States into complacency. These individuals are also concerned with the apparent national "loss of will" resulting from the Vietnam War and the increased public pressure for decreases in military spending. The ultraconservatives are arms advocates who believe in a strong military and a U.S. global strategy that supports intervention when and where American interests are threatened.

In areas of economic policy, the ultraconservatives are particularly alarmed by the decline of the United States as a producer of goods and services and by the concomitant rise of Japan, Western Europe, and newly industrialized Asian countries such as South Korea, Hong Kong, and Malaysia. The loss of markets to these new competitors and the increasing amount of foreign investment in the United States has caused many groups to advocate more protectionist legislation and the implementation of rules prohibiting or, at minimum, limiting foreign ownership of U.S. property. These nationalistic and neomercantilist pressures collide with the "laissez faire" philosophy, which defines the international economic order essentially established by the United States after World War II. The Bretton Woods System encourages states to limit public interventions in the marketplace and rely on free- or fair-trade practices. Thus, global educators who teach about cooperation and joint economic ventures (e.g., a Toyota-General Motors automobile) are simply describing adjustments within the Bretton Woods system. However, for many groups on the extreme right, the U.S. goal should be economic hegemony—a return to the immediate post-World War II era of U.S. economic and political dominance. Most would disagree with David Calleo's (1982) proposition that the rise of economic competitors is a natural outgrowth of U.S. policy aimed at helping the world recover from World War II. Calleo also suggests that today's more pluralistic economic system should be seen not as an indicator of U.S. decline, but as a victory for the competitive system implemented by the United States.

As one would expect, the ultraconservatives are looking to someone to blame for this loss of economic power. Unfortunately, the target has become foreign corporations and citizens from some of the more successful economic markets. Racism and xenophobia against Asians has increased dramatically throughout the United States. The ultraconservatives seem to want a return to autarky, or self-reliance, if they cannot have a world market controlled by the Americans. Most don't seem to understand the shift (described in Chapter 1 by Lee Anderson) from national economies, where nationally based industries trade among each other, to a global economy, where financial and production processes for a single product are distributed among a number of countries. In a global market, it is difficult to identify one's enemies and target countries for retaliation. For example, if the United States decided to limit products exported from Taiwan, this action would hurt two U.S.-based corporations—RCA and AT&T—two of the top four exporters from this country (Reich 1988). The decline in U.S. hegemony has produced many frustrations associated with a loss of income, status, and power; and many people who have suffered such losses find it difficult to see these issues comprehensively. The search for scapegoats rather than solutions is usually the result.

In the schools, reformists who teach about cooperation in a multinational marketplace, who encourage the study of other cultures, and who welcome the increasing cultural diversity in our communities are often criticized for teaching "one worldism" and for suggesting that other societies are morally and politically equivalent to the United States. This emphasis on "moral equivalence" is considered unpatriotic and is seen as undermining attempts at building loyal Americans. For more conservative interest groups, teaching patriotism is the primary purpose of schooling. This idea that U.S. policymakers are always correct and should not be criticized by an uninformed public may result in further losses of power, prestige, influence, and markets in a global economy and a more pluralistic international political environment.

It is clear that much of the support for ultraconservatives is a result of frustrations associated with the loss of power and influence in the international system and very real domestic implications (e.g., loss of jobs to foreign manufacturers), which require costly adjustments in economic systems. The United States is no longer the hegemon, but a major power in a more pluralistic system. By wishing for the past and refusing to recognize very real changes in the international system, the ultraconservatives are irresponsibly attempting to deny American students an education that will enable them to compete, cooperate, and live peacefully at home and abroad.

Earlier, I suggested that another explanation for the global education controversy could be attributed to a "more reformist orientation" among those supporters of global education. Their more change-oriented belief system conflicts with status-quo forces in the schools and the community.

Many teachers are attracted to the "social engineering" aspects of the profession. They are convinced that they can help shape the future by helping to prepare the successor generation. These teachers see the chance to do something about persistent social problems faced by their students. Any review of the backgrounds of teachers interested in global education would reveal a well-informed population that is receptive to policy strategies promoting system reforms and addressing problems like poverty, pollution, conflict, and abuses of human rights. Educators who are active in global education programs tend to belong to policy-oriented interest groups (e.g., Sierra Club and Amnesty International) and are more likely to have read about an issue or attended a conference or enrolled in a course to learn more about an international issue. Their interest and spirit of activism far exceed the public norm.

This is not to say that all teachers are well informed and adequately prepared to teach global issues. Many make poor teaching choices and simply present one side of an issue or design entire courses around normative goals that correspond to their worldview. This is polemics, not instruction. Advocacy-oriented educators deserve to be criticized. Yet, one polemical reformist agenda should not be replaced by a more conservative vision of what ought to be.

As government becomes more involved in our private lives and as more public funds are used for educational programs, public interest will increase. The public agenda is growing exponentially, and as more issues are "politicized" the chances for controversy increase. The more status-quo oriented public is growing more cautious about any change-oriented views. Some tend to be more attracted by the core assumptions of ultraconservatives who offer simple and permanent solutions. They promise a return to greatness if we go back to basics and rediscover the traditions, values, and political beliefs that made us great. The success of the Reagan administration in convincing the American people that they could return to a position of preeminence, the "eagle-resurgent" argument, suggests that many U.S. citizens are attracted by this worldview.

The more reformist global educators' position was best represented by the early months of the Carter administration. During this time, President Carter urged Americans to see the world as more pluralistic and complex. He urged American citizens to abandon their preoccupation with U.S.-Soviet issues and recognize the need to respond to global poverty, human rights abuses, the depletion of natural resources, and persistent conflicts throughout the world. Carter was quickly dismissed as naive and idealistic. His calls for cooperation were labeled as "appeasement"; his insistence on developing an appreciation for the global commons and his endorsement of a multilateral limiting of growth earned him the label of President Gloom and Doom. Many educators and members of the public are still convinced that President Carter was actually calling for a foreign policy based on multilateralism, demilitarization, depolarization, and a recognition of global responsibility and accountability (Brown 1984). It is rather obvious that this view would challenge the dominant neomercantilist view—as well as the ultraconservative image—of how things ought to be. These clashing images of reality continue to fuel the controversy over global education in the schools.

This controversy is also a dispute over the role schools should play in the political education of young people. The extremists on the right are supportive of a more traditional educational agenda that focuses on U.S. history, state and local government, U.S. politics, Western Civilization, and free-trade economics. They believe that students should be prepared to be American citizens and to represent American interests in a competitive international environment. They are critical of global educators' emphasis on the inevitability of system change; the assumption that change will lead to more international and intercultural interdependence; and the implication that a global system requires more emphasis on transnational values, critical thinking, and comparative analysis. Ultraconservatives imply that new courses will be offered at the expense of the aforementioned traditional curriculum. The conservatives feel that the hidden agenda is a move toward world government, a rejection of the state system, and an emphasis on multiple loyalties and cultural relativism that will undermine our society.

It is clear to most educators that there is some merit in both approaches. Our political culture changes as the realities of political life change. Thus, our process of political thinking or political socialization will have to adjust to new circumstances in international politics. This does not mean abandoning the past, nor does it mean ignoring transformations that challenge some of our core assumptions and require some new thinking. To illustrate, many Americans continue to revere the nation-state and insist on policymaking sovereignty in a world where many of the issues are transnational. These issues, however, do not respect political or geographic boundaries—and they cannot be fully resolved by the actions of a single state. The member states of the European Community may be introducing all of us to a future system of governance as they prepare to coordinate policies, share resources and expertise, and surrender policymaking authority to a single market community in 1992. The European integration process has not been easy; however, consider that some of these countries were major antagonists in two world wars. Perhaps the United States might learn some lessons from our European allies.

It may be necessary for U.S. educators to rethink some of the basics of political socialization. For example, are highly competitive strategies (i.e., win at any cost) appropriate in a world that is connected by complex economic, political, and cultural linkages? The entire global education controversy may be about an unwillingness to revise our thinking about how we conduct foreign policy in a more pluralistic system. Americans have not adjusted to the change in status from rulemaker in most policy areas to ruletaker in many areas. U.S. national security may no longer be defined by dominance, control, and the insecurity of others. In the contemporary international system, U.S. security and power may be defined by America's ability to work in concert with others to solve persistent global problems and its ability to see that insecurity of other states is a greater threat to U.S. security and the security of the global community.

Implications for Teacher Preparation

It is not enough to say that teachers should present all sides of a controversial issue (Lamy 1989). The simple truth is that most teachers are not prepared to do that. Policy statements about the need for balance do not respond to the major problem: There are too few opportunities for educators to enroll in courses that introduce them to relevant theoretical and policy-related information on international affairs. How can educators present all sides of an issue when they are not well informed about contending views? The CHI program is one of about ten university-school collaboratives that offer inservice global education programs for K-12 educators. (In Chapter 7, Jan Tucker describes the characteristics of successful partnerships in global education.) Even so, these programs are making only a small impact on America's teacher and student populations. More needs to be done at the preservice and inservice levels. Universities need to begin creating collaborative teacher preparation programs in which courses are team taught or cooperatively designed by specialists in curriculum and instruction and specialists in international affairs. One cannot assume that students who plan on becoming teachers will bring the knowledge gained in their required world history course to their teaching methods class. We must see the connections.

For example, the University of Southern California offers a program in teaching contemporary international issues. The course is designed for people who want to explore these issues and appropriate classroom teaching ideas. Each issue module (e.g., the politics of international trade) within the course presents participants with:

1. A comprehensive and thorough discussion of significant data and theoretical debates that define the issue.

2. A careful analysis of explanations used to account for the development of an issue or event.

3. A review of teaching materials and resources developed for classroom use in the subject area.

4. A creative discussion focusing on how best to "adapt" the research on complex international issues for teaching purposes.

5. Appropriate information-gathering strategies to encourage students and their teachers to continue gathering relevant data from ideological, gender-related, historical, and cultural sources.

6. A sharing of ideas and strategies to enable the teacher participants to disseminate this new information to colleagues and students.

This sort of program may not provide all of the answers and may not resolve present or future controversies. Yet, in a world where controversy rules, it is critically important to discuss the issues that cause concern. Teachers and their students must be prepared to see each issue from a variety of worldviews and then, after this critical assessment, make their choices. These choices will shape their future and the future of others in distant lands.

References

Brown, S. (Winter 1984). "New Forces Revisited: Lessons of a Turbulent Decade." *World Policy Journal* 1: 397-418.

Calleo, D. (1982). *The Imperious Economy*. Cambridge: Harvard University Press.

Cunningham, G. (1986). "Blowing the Whistle on Global Education." Unpublished report. Washington, D.C.: U.S. Department of Education, Region VII.

Fitzgerald, F. (May 10, 1987). "Reagan's Band of True Believers." *New York Times Magazine*, 36.

Hanvey, R. (1976). *An Attainable Global Perspective*. Denver, Colo.: Center for Teaching International Relations.

Keohane, R., and J. Nye. (1989) *Power and Independence*. Boston: Scott, Foresman.

Lamy, S. (1987). *The Definition of a Discipline: The Objects and Methods of Analysis in Global Education*. New York: Global Perspectives in Education.

Lamy, S., ed. (1988). *Contemporary International Issues*. Boulder, Colo.: Lynne Rienner Publishers.

Lamy, S. (Spring 1989). "Controversy in the Social Studies Classroom: A Review of Concerns Related to Teaching International Relations." *International Journal of Social Education*.

Maghrooi, R., and B. Ramberg. (1982). *Globalism Versus Realism*. Boulder, Colo.: Westview Press.

Reich, R. (February 12, 1988). "The Trade Gap: Myths and Crocodile Tears." *New York Times*, 27.

Ryerson, A. (May 13, 1988). "The Ticking Bomb of Nuclear Age Education." *The Wall Street Journal*, n.p.

Schafly, P. (March 6, 1986). "What Is Wrong With Global Education." *St. Louis Democrat*, n.p.

Vasquez, J., ed. (1986). *Classics of International Relations*. Englewood Cliffs, N.J.: Prentice Hall.

Part II
Practice

4

Curriculum Considerations in Global Studies

James Becker

Americans are increasingly recognizing that our lives and hopes for the future are linked to events and developments around the world. This recognition has created a variety of positive responses from political leaders, educators, and ordinary citizens. The National Governors' Association, meeting in New York in December 1987, called a global perspective a "key to prosperity." In 1989, the governors recommended that global, international, and foreign language education become part of the basic education for all students and that each state take action to expand their international programs. A report released in 1987 by a study commission made up of nationally known educators, including Clark Kerr, President Emeritus, University of California; Harlan Cleveland, Dean, Hubert H. Humphrey Institute of Public Affairs; and John I. Goodlad, Director, Center for Educational Renewal, University of Washington, recommended a nationwide, intensive effort to improve and expand global education in the nation's schools.

The annual *State of the World* reports (Worldwatch Institute 1989), perhaps the most complete, up-to-date, readily available reference on the world's resources, provide further evidence that effective citizenship today requires a global perspective. The authors note that meeting the needs of our society, without diminishing the prospects of future generations, can be accomplished only if a sufficient number of citizens are well informed and concerned about global issues.

If people are to respond to the changing world conditions described by Lee Anderson in Chapter 1 of this book, they must cross what Harvard

University professor Harvey Brooks called "perceptual thresholds" (quoted by Lester Brown 1987, xvi). That is, enough people must see the situation, or threat, if a cogent response is to occur. Information, knowledge, and understanding are essential to crossing such thresholds.

The information and concern that spark a response may come in dramatic form, such as the nuclear power accidents at Three Mile Island and Chernobyl or the energy crises of the '70s. But such events are likely to result in effective, desirable action only when citizens are prepared to see them in a global context. The United States cannot deal effectively with international economic, political, and environmental issues without developing greater international competence among our citizens. U.S. educational institutions and organizations must broaden citizens' training in communicating with other people; understanding other cultures; and recognizing relationships among population growth, rising standards of living, and environmental problems.

Because of the increasing internationalization of society and interdependence among peoples and nations, citizenship education—a traditional and essential component of education in the United States—must have a global dimension. The subtle connections that link an individual's daily life with global systems provide new opportunities to learn about world affairs and participate in them. These conditions also require new knowledge, skills, and sensitivities. Increasingly, it is necessary for U.S. citizens to embrace simultaneously a local, national, and global perspective. The ability of the United States to provide leadership in our rapidly changing world depends on the attitudes and behavior of the general citizenry. Public values and perceptions place limits on and help define the actions of political leaders.

As Lee Anderson has made clear in Chapter 1 of this book, the impact of international trade, foreign investment, tourism, immigration, and cultural exchanges is felt today in virtually every local community. The tremendous increase in transnational interactions has ramifications for the daily lives of all citizens. Moreover, such interconnectedness promises to be a permanent feature of tomorrow's world. We have reached a point in the world's history and the history of our nation in which the field of international/global studies has become an essential aspect of school curriculums, rather than a temporary response to a real or presumed crisis. Given this circumstance, the global dimensions of current curriculum offerings need to be improved and expanded.

Indeed, a complete restructuring of existing school policies and curriculums may be desirable; but this chapter focuses on a much less ambitious goal: suggesting some ways of adding an international dimension to selected, widely available courses in American elementary and secondary schools. The need to improve and expand international content and perspectives in all curriculum areas is acknowledged, but the examples and suggestions here are limited largely to the social studies.

The Status Quo

Recent studies (Gross 1977, Jarolimek 1977, Morrissett 1986, Shaver, Davis, and Helburn 1979) indicate that the dominant structure of secondary social studies today is remarkably similar to a pattern set in 1916. (Such a pattern is an example of what Barbara Tye, in Chapter 2, calls the "deep structure" of schooling.) Based on state and local requirements, course enrollments, and what teachers teach, as well as what schools offer, the following pattern of social studies courses (listed by grade level) predominates today:

1. Families
2. Neighborhoods
3. Communities
4. State history/regions
5. U.S. history
6. World history/western hemisphere
7. World history/cultures/geography
8. U.S. history
9. Civics/government or world culture/history
10. World cultures/history
11. U.S. history
12. American government and economics or sociology/psychology

The social studies curriculum in most secondary schools is organized around topics (places, continents, and subjects) that were established 60 years ago. Over the years, changes in the content of that curriculum have been made, and variations and exceptions to specific courses at particular grade levels exist throughout the United States. Generally, however, the topics, courses, and textbooks are remarkably similar across the nation.

The most notable changes since 1916 include the broadening of European history to world history, with more emphasis on Africa, Asia, and other non-western areas. Ninth grade civics has in some cases given ground to world history. Economics is a more frequently offered course at the 12th grade, and a course called "problems of democracy" has become a course in American government. Many schools also offer electives such as economics, sociology, and psychology.

U.S. history is the most pervasive course taught throughout the country. Textbooks emphasizing chronological surveys of U.S. history are widely used in these courses. A few social studies programs are being taught on the basis of other themes, such as skills, student development needs, or social issues.

International studies receives scant attention, other than in world geography and world history courses, where the emphasis tends to be on geographic areas or regions or, as in the case of world history, a chronology of major events in the western world. World cultures, global studies, and international relations may be offered in a growing number of secondary schools, but enrollment is small. For most students, an acquaintance with the postindustrial, technologically intertwined, complex world system of today is limited to what they learn in U.S. history or American government.

For example, students receive little or no instruction in the role of multinational corporations in the production, processing, and distribution of major products or agricultural commodities; the involvement of states in promoting trade and foreign investment; and the importance of cooperation and competition among the world's major trading partners. High school social studies courses seldom provide extensive discussions of international organizations such as the United Nations, the European Community, the World Council of Churches, NATO, or the thousands of other agencies through which individuals and groups help shape the postindustrial world.

Recommended Changes

Charting a Course: Social Studies for the 21st Century, a report of the National Commission on Social Studies in the Schools (1989), recommends a number of changes in the traditional pattern of social studies courses. World history and world geography are given greater attention. The authors also suggest that U.S. history might be taught in the context of world history. Nevertheless, by emphasizing a chronological approach to history and a study of place geography, the Commission's proposed curriculum for the 21st century is much like current social studies programs. Charting a course for 21st century social studies requires a vision of a preferred future. The Commission report failed to provide a vision of what future citizens or society should seek to achieve; rather, the authors focused mainly on how the academic disciplines should divide the time allocated to the social studies.

Preparing students for living in a more pluralistic, intertwined, international system requires new competencies and skills that are interdisciplinary and not culture and time bound. Students need to be exposed to information from a variety of cultural, ideological, and gender-related perspectives. They also need opportunities to learn skills that will enable them to analyze problems, evaluate contending policy positions, and take effective action to change conditions that threaten life on planet Earth.

Education for democratic citizenship in a global age calls for a new look at our past and a greater concern for our future. We need to find out how to meet the current needs of the world's people without jeopardizing the prospects of our children and grandchildren. We must recognize that it is in our interest to work for the survival of the species as a whole and for the actualization—in the greatest possible number of individuals—of their potential for good will, intelligence, and creativity. Narrow nationalism, dogmatic ideologies, and an endangered environment are luxuries humans can no longer afford. There must be a shift from the politics dominated by rampant nationalism and military power to the problems of the human species and human ecology. Current reform efforts in the social studies fail to address these overriding concerns.

Until such time as the long-established pattern of courses changes, classroom teachers and social studies specialists need to learn how best to use existing courses and curriculums to help students acquire an international perspective. Students and teachers alike need to learn how to interpret human interactions in a larger context, including a wider range of human experience. For example, social studies courses should provide for the study of the history and environmental conditions of *all* human beings and cultures, not just male heroes, wars, and western civilization.

Recently, many attempts have been made to improve and expand international studies in schools. Several curriculum areas have been involved—language studies, the natural sciences, and the humanities—but most have probably involved social studies. These efforts include the following:

• The introduction into the curriculum of more content focused on Asia, Africa, and Latin America, combined with efforts to reduce western bias in teaching about the non-West.

• Special projects and programs that provide materials and services on topics such as energy, peace, conflict, population, economic development, and trade.

• More attention to world geography and world history.

• More offerings in economics, with some recognition of its global context.

• Recommendations by several states that schools place increased emphasis on global studies.

• More "outreach activities" for many of the Title 6, U.S. Department of Education, National Resource Centers for Area and International Studies.

Despite the increased attention that international studies are receiving at the national, state, and local levels, there has probably been little change in the content or methods being used in most classrooms. We have not paid enough attention to involving teachers at the school level in acquiring new insights and information. Only now are programs beginning to be developed, such as the program at the Center for Human Interdependence (CHI) at Chapman College in Orange County, California. CHI programs and others aim to improve global curriculum content and to facilitate the processes of change, including providing time for teachers to work together to review, rethink, and revitalize their courses.

State-Level Educational Reforms and Global Education

School reform has become a prominent and persistent feature on state policy agendas. Governors, state legislatures, and chief state school officers cooperate or vie with one another over matters of educational policy. The Council of State Governments and the National Governors' Association (NGA) have given education, including international education, high priority on their agendas. In 1985, the Council of Chief State School Officers issued a major report that strongly endorsed international education and foreign language programs.

Several states, including New Jersey, California, Massachusetts, Florida, Minnesota, New York, and Washington, have passed resolutions, created positions, and appropriated money for global/international education. Legislation supporting similar efforts is pending in several other states. Some states have published guidelines or curriculums for global or international education. (See "State and Local Guidelines" at the end of this chapter.)

The rationales for many of the state efforts exhibit similar arguments. Typical is *Increasing International and Intercultural Competence through the Social Sciences*, available from the Illinois State Board of Education:

> It becomes increasingly imperative that schools equip students to participate effectively in a highly interdependent and culturally diverse world. . . . It is a world in which individuals, local communities, and states conduct "foreign policies and foreign relations" as they provide famine relief to people on distant continents and court foreign investors and markets for locally produced goods.

The Illinois statement includes the following goals for students to pursue in the social sciences:

- Understand and analyze comparative political economic systems, with an emphasis on the political and economic systems of the United States.
- Understand and analyze events, trends, personalities, and movements shaping the history of the world, the United States, and Illinois.
- Demonstrate a knowledge of the basic concepts of the social sciences and how these help to interpret human behavior.
- Demonstrate a knowledge of world geography with emphasis on that of the United States.
- Apply the skills and knowledge gained in the social sciences to decision making in life situations.

Another state guideline, *Missouri in the World*, published by the Missouri Department of Elementary and Secondary Education in 1986 and distributed to every school in the state, includes the following statement:

> Interaction among Missourians and people from other nations and cultures has become increasingly frequent and significant in recent decades. This interaction—the result of tourism, church missions, international trade, professional conferences, improved communication, international politics, and educational and artistic exchange—has widespread implications for the quality of life in the state and for the education of our youth.

A bill introduced in the State of New York Assembly in March 1988 includes the following assertion:

> The prosperity of New York state will, to an increasing degree, depend on a citizenry with skills and sensitivities to deal with a rapidly changing and internationally interdependent world. . . . [It is] imperative that students learn about the languages and histories of other cultures and nations to be better prepared for employment in the increasingly internationally competitive world of the future.

In recent years, one state, California, has published guidelines that include a global perspective. For example, *Model Curriculum Standards: Grades Nine Through Twelve* (1985), includes the following statement: "Knowledge is not simply factual data or skills taught in isolation. It is a body of concepts and processes which enables us to understand our development as citizens in an increasingly diverse and interdependent world."

The 1987 California *History-Social Science Framework* has been analyzed for its compatibility with and support for global/international themes. Staff members of CHI and of the Immaculate Heart College in Los Angeles have concluded that an awareness of the importance of global perspectives pervades the California framework. It is a landmark set of guidelines for school-based curriculum development that can be used to promote citizen understanding of our increasingly diverse and interdependent world. For example, the social studies section of the framework states:

> A course in world history, culture, and geography . . . should strive to illuminate the cultural, economic, geographic and political interactions of peoples and cultures over time. Only by keeping this in sight will students grasp the deep historical roots of contemporary global interdependence.

Diane Ravitch (1989), an historian of education at Teachers College, Columbia University, cites the framework "as a compelling model that deserves broad attention." She also notes that "in this enthusiasm for international studies California has not lost sight of its responsibility for preparing young people to be active and informed citizens of the United States." Asserting that "we have much to gain by learning about other cultures and . . . they have much to gain by learning about ours," Ravitch cautions: "Learning about other people does not require us to relinquish our values."

The changes recommended in state guidelines and mandates generally call for more emphasis on world areas or cultures, as well as world history or geography. Few of them deal with the concept of global systems in a manner that might shed light on what a Japanese industrialist has called the "borderless world economy" or global environmental concerns, such as depletion of the ozone layer, acid rain, or pollution of the oceans.

The publicity surrounding state mandates, state legislation, and the highly visible political activities involved make such efforts important, because they demonstrate a shift in the "deep structure" of schooling described by Barbara Tye in Chapter 2. State control of teacher training and certification, student testing, and curriculum content influences school practice. However, as many past state-initiated efforts have demonstrated, unless state leadership succeeds in mobilizing local efforts, these highly visible measures have limited influence. Enacting reforms is easier than improving school performance. The success of reform efforts ultimately depends on the improvements made at the school level.

Curriculums with a Global Perspective

The increasingly global character of human experience is evident in changes in emphasis of the various academic disciplines. Curriculums in the arts, languages, sciences, and social studies are changing in a variety of ways; and teachers who are interested in bringing a global perspective to their programs, particularly in the social studies, do not have to start from scratch. There are a number of curriculum developments to which they can turn, some of which are reviewed here.

World Studies Approaches

Many projects and proposals that seek to improve and expand global studies in schools emphasize an infusion of international studies throughout the curriculum. Such efforts can play a vital role in helping break down artificial boundaries between the disciplines as well as between domestic and international affairs. However, there are limits to the infusion strategy.

A sound world studies course can offer a more systematic, integrated approach to understanding the world. The need for new approaches to world geography, world history, and world cultures is widely recognized. The challenge, however, is in conceptualizing and implementing a course that is easily taught, academically sound, and politically acceptable to both teachers and community groups.

An increasing number of states and many local school districts are reinstating or adding world history or global studies as a recommended or mandated part of their curriculum. In many cases this course represents the only opportunity students have, after the seventh grade, to study the world in a systematic way.

A practical look at several approaches to organizing a high school world studies curriculum can be found in Woyach and Remy (1988). These authors outline an approach to world history that emphasizes the study of change on a global scale, and they call for studies in world geography, historical cultures, and international relations. Each approach deals with interdependence, economic development, complexity, change, and historical perspective. The advantages and disadvantages, a rationale, goals, and suggested topics are listed with each approach. Also included is a chapter on program evaluation that offers guidelines for assessing each approach.

Focus on the World: The Role of History

The College Entrance Examination Board (1986), in its *Academic Preparation in Social Studies*, states the case well for global studies: "The social studies curriculum should be augmented and refined, taking into account new findings in social history, by adopting a worldwide prospective, and by incorporating social science concepts more thoroughly."

The College Board included the following recommendations regarding the teaching of world history, geography, and cultures:

> The topic here is the world, not each and every one of its constituent parts. The focus is on developments that are of the largest significance to the whole of civilizations.... Teaching about the history of the world must proceed top down, deductively employing ways in which events and developments of the past can be grouped together as communalities, continuities and contrasts.... The movement of traditional to modern societies, the spread of the most widely shared religions and languages and the still developing worldwide shift to industrial economics are ... significant developments with which world history is concerned.

History, with its well-established place in the social studies curriculum, can be a vehicle for understanding the realities of today's world. However, not all approaches to the study of history make valuable contributions to the development of international perspectives. Some approaches to history promote ethnocentrism and are destructive of an international frame of reference. For example, in the United States, courses in world history usually focus on the history of Western Civilization, with a hodgepodge of separate discussions of geographic or cultural areas tacked on. Such a focus on western culture, accompanied by fragmented views of other cultures, often undercuts the most significant contributions of a study of world history—the understanding of interrelationships between peoples, countries, and continents. The newly formed World History Association holds this view, and its future contributions should be of great value.

An increasing number of comparative and regional histories go beyond the study of a single nation or culture and identify crucial concepts or ideas that are common to two or more nations, cultures, or peoples. Properly used, the comparative approach powerfully highlights the communalities in human experience and in the historical development of nations and cultures. When students begin to see that the history of their own nation or region has similarities to that of other peoples, the students can begin to draw parallels and make analogies. Such approaches also help students understand the significance of Edwin Reischauer's (1976) argument:

> The history we must know is not what we once assumed it to be—it is not just our own national past and its cultural background in early modern Europe, medieval Christendom, Rome and Greece, with the history of other people included only to the extent of our contact with them. History, to be relevant today . . . must encompass as much as possible of the total experience of mankind.

Leften Stavrianos (1964) has described another approach to global history: "It means the perspective of an observer perched on the moon rather than ensconced in London or Paris or Washington. It means that for every period of history, we are interested in events and movements of global rather than regional or national significance."

William McNeill (1979) emphasizes the role of cultural diffusion in history. By giving attention to the diffusion of food crops, military technologies, political systems, and disease, he highlights the interrelationships and shared cultural developments—the common heritage of humankind.

In "What History for the Year 2000?" T.H. Von Laue (1981) calls for a new civic history with a

> . . . keen moral sensibility for all humanity (as well as its natural habitat). . . . It proceeds from a lively awareness . . . . of human interactions on which the material existence of the . . . five or six billion human beings in the world depends. The framework runs, for our American students, all the way from neighborhood, to state, region, nation, hemisphere and innumerable multinational institutions . . . to the globe.

The typical course of study in U.S. schools provides little understanding of the rise and decline of nations, especially as these general patterns of history relate to the changing place of the United States in the global system. To acquire such insights, most American citizens must put aside their ethnocentric views. The heavy dose of U.S. history found in most American schools largely ignores the changing nature of the world system and the changing role of the United States in that system. Unfortunately, the ability to recite the names of the presidents in chronological order or to show an intimate knowledge of the Constitution or the Missouri Compromise is not of much help to citizens in understanding how the world is changing.

History without a global context cannot really help today's citizens understand how their country developed and where it may be heading in an increasingly interconnected world. Global history incorporates a knowledge of the larger economic, historical, and strategic changes that have occurred over the past centuries. As Paul Kennedy (1988), Dilworth Professor of History at Yale University, notes: "You only properly understand your own country when you remove the ethnocentric spectacles, examine the history of other countries, and put your own nation within the larger context of global development." (See also Kennedy 1987 for a comprehensive study of economic and military issues in the past five centuries.)

"International history" can also be used to broaden students' perspectives. This approach exposes students to topics as they are seen in other nations. For example, the Ministry of Education of Japan (n.d.) has prepared a variety of materials relating to international history, including *As Others See Us* and *Verdict on America*. These materials can help students learn to detect biases, including their own, and to obtain a different perspective on events traditionally included in U.S. or world history courses.

Some examples of instructional materials based on a global approach to history include works by Stavrianos (1979), David Weitzman and Richard Gross (1977), John Thompson and Kathleen Hedberg (1977), and McNeill (1973, 1979).

A growing volume of material from other countries and from organizations such as UNESCO (see Graves, Dunlap, and Torney-Purta 1984; Mehlinger 1981), the Council of Europe (1989), and the National Council for the Social Studies (Mehlinger and Tucker 1979) demonstrates the manner in which other nations are seeking to enhance international perspectives. (See also *Europe Today* [1985], which includes maps that can be reproduced.)

Economics and Global Education

Concern in government and business circles over huge international trade deficits has resulted in dozens of reports on international competitiveness. Though these reports focus primarily on business considerations and government policies in support of business, the role of education receives some attention. There is growing recognition that our basic resource is an educated and skilled people. Such a view suggests that a main component of economic competitiveness is educational competitiveness; what we can do in the global economy is shaped by what we know. Further, the belief is that U.S. citizens must have knowledge and skills at least equal to those of our competitors. Citizens must understand the global economy that touches all our lives and raises crucial issues of public policy.

Economics is receiving more attention in the nation's classrooms. Economic literacy in the 1990s requires that citizens understand how national, regional, and personal well being is influenced by the world economy. World trade, immigration (legal and illegal), soybean sales, tourism, currency exchanges, and drug smuggling are examples of activities that take place in the global economy. In addition, multinational corporations have the capacity to shift jobs as well as billions of dollars of assets across national boundaries. Like foreign investment and trade deficits, all these activities touch the lives of people in every community in the United States.

77

As Lee Anderson points out in Chapter 1, we need to be aware of the increasing role of state governments, state and local business groups, and community organizations in promoting foreign investment, tourism, and the sale abroad of products grown or produced within the state. These developments are expanding the numbers of individuals and groups involved in transnational interactions. The Center for Innovative Diplomacy (1988-89) has provided many examples of the growing international involvement of local and state groups.

Unfortunately, few U.S. citizens are prepared to deal with the "worldwide involvements of daily life" (Alger 1987). The study of local and state roles in international economic transactions is a promising way to make explicit the variety of ways that ordinary people in towns, cities, and rural areas are immersed in worldwide activities. The links between daily life of local places in different countries—and between these places and world power centers— need to be made explicit. A major effort to delineate these connections and assess their impact can be found in *Columbus in the World* (Mershon Center 1976). Several states and local communities have produced materials designed to identify and assess the impact of their connections and transactions with other nations and peoples. (See "State and Local Guidelines"; see also Remy and Woyach 1983.)

Other groups with global perspectives offer guidelines and resources for a study of global economics. The Joint Council on Economic Education has recently produced some publications designed to strengthen the international dimensions of economic literacy. The Foreign Policy Association (1988; see also Cutler 1978) offers works on world trade and employment; this association includes other relevant topics in its *Great Decisions* program. The World Bank (1988) publishes economic statistics for 125 countries, as well as case studies of Kenya and Mexico. Other useful World Bank resources are *Toward a Better World* (1981), a multimedia kit on economic development, and a series of poster kits (1989). Both the Social Science Education Consortium (Switzer and Mulloy 1987) and the Joint Council on Economic Education (1980, 1988) publish curricular guides and teaching resources in global economics. Other materials suitable for adding international dimension to economics courses or units include "The World Economy: An Overview" (National Council for the Social Studies 1984) and *The World Economy and the Multinational Corporation* (1984).

Global Geography

Geography has been making a comeback in many schools across the United States. Recent surveys have demonstrated major deficiencies in student knowledge of the regions where the students live; and publicity given these results has sparked a number of new programs and projects. The Association of American Geographers and the National Council for Geographic

Education (1984) have jointly prepared guidelines for the study of geography. The National Geographic Society (1986) distributes map posters illustrating these guidelines and provides ideas, suggestions, and recommendations relating to improving and expanding geographic education.

In these publications, themes such as location, place, human environment, and interactions are used to demonstrate the importance of geography in promoting student understanding of the complex environments of the Earth and their interdependence. Thus, students can see how decisions made at one location or place might affect people and the environment elsewhere. Geographic knowledge is cited as crucial in dealing with many of today's major problems—nuclear arms buildups, inequitable distribution of economic resources, the resettlement of refugees, and terrorism.

Many of the ideas and recommendations in these reports are essential elements in the development of global geography. Alan Backler (see Backler and Stoltman 1988), a widely respected geographic educator, states: "Global geography provides young people with perspectives, information, concepts and skills essential to understanding themselves, their relationship to the earth, and their interdependence with other peoples of the world . . . reinforces and extends the processes of critical thinking and problem solving that are applicable to all parts of the curriculum" (p. 4). He believes global geography can help young people understand that absolute and relative location are important aspects of every natural and cultural feature on earth.

Backler cites five goals of instruction in global geography as helping students achieve the following:

1. Understand that absolute and relative location are significant aspects of every natural and cultural feature on earth. . . . Knowing the absolute location of Afghanistan and its location relative to that of the Islamic minorities in the U.S.S.R. can help students understand recent events in that country.
2. Be able to determine the significance of places in terms of their natural and human characteristics and determine how the meaning of places changes over time.
3. Be aware of different ways in which people inhabit, modify, and adapt culturally to natural environments.
4. Examine how places are interdependent and the implications of that interdependence.
5. Learn to use the concept of region as a tool. . . . Students will be able to use the concept of region to identify areas of the world where firewood is a major energy resource . . . and describe and evaluate the human and environmental features found in these parts of the world (Backler 1986).

Geography all too often has treated the world as a collection of isolated nations or regions. The increasing interconnectedness as evidenced by widespread use of the same technology by peoples in all areas of the world is creating a new emphasis on geography. The new geographic agenda parallels many of the concerns of global education. Examples of new approaches in geography are a textbook, *Global Geography* (Backler and Hanvey 1986), and a series of videotapes with the same title (Agency for Instructional Technology 1988).

Interdisciplinary Courses and Materials Needed

The many opportunities available to integrate an international perspective into existing, discipline-focused courses should not blind us to the fact that many of the issues and events that demand our attention lend themselves to interdisciplinary approaches. Improved understanding of key issues such as food, energy, pollution, defense and security, resource use, and human rights, for example, probably requires an approach that goes beyond the treatment offered within a single discipline. Current issues that have enduring importance are an attractive basis for organizing a global studies course. Students are likely to be interested in events happening now that have clear relevance to their own concerns. Properly treated, such issues can help students to acquire key concepts, such as development, security, sustainable growth, and comparative advantage, as they are used by international relations experts. The following criteria by Woyach and Remy are helpful in selecting such issues:

1. The issue should be of worldwide, not merely a U.S. concern.
2. The issue should involve problems that require action by more than one nation. The opportunity to examine the basis of international conflict and cooperation should be paramount in this regard.
3. The issue should enable students to gain a historical perspective on not only the issue but in the development of the international system.
4. The issue should also make apparent basic characteristics of the international system (Woyach and Remy 1988, 171-177).

Among the many possible issues for study are the search for security in a nuclear age; the challenge of gaps between rich and poor nations; and the environmental concerns related to population growth, resource depletion, and deterioration of the ecosphere. Traditionally, these issues have been viewed as foreign policy concerns of major nations of the world. The power-politics approach focuses largely on the cooperation among the larger nations. Given the changing nature of today's world, it would seem appropriate to broaden our focus and look at patterns of interaction among various peoples, cultures, governments, and nongovernmental organizations. We should emphasize key characteristics of the world system and the behavior of a variety of international groups—governments, multinational corporations, the United Nations, and regional economic or military groups. This emphasis will help students understand the structure as well as the changing nature of the international system. The states of Wisconsin, New York, Illinois, and California offer useful guidelines for such offerings. (See "State and Local Guidelines.") Another related work is *American History and National Security* (1987), published by the Mershon Center, Ohio State University.

Cooperative Learning and Global Education

Radical shifts in our economy and the increasingly pluralistic nature of our population are forcing a reexamination of what and how we teach. The trend toward an information-based, high-technology, interdependent, rapidly chang-ing economy supports the need for teaching high-level thinking skills, as well as the communication and social skills necessary for participation in the increasingly interdependent world. Racial, linguistic, economic, and social diversity calls for teaching methods that accommodate heterogeneity in proficiency levels and cultural backgrounds.

The heart of complex organizational life today is collaboration. Words like "we" and "our" replace "I" and "my." The team, not the leader, is viewed as the key to success. Collaboration generates the best ideas and options for running an organization. Allan Cox (1989), a highly respected management consultant, claims that "corporations that do not think teamwork, will not prosper." It may seem contradictory, but our hopes to become more competi-tive in an increasingly interdependent world may well require more emphasis on cooperation.

The world is not just competitive—and in some important respects, it probably must become less so. For example, in many organizations, job-related skills may not be as crucial as interpersonal skills.

The increasingly complex, unpredictable, changing world requires stu-dents to be prepared to be flexible so they can recognize and adopt to cooperative, competitive, and individualistic social interactions. It is foolish to prepare students to be only competitive or only cooperative. More attention needs to be given to recent developments in learning, which stress collabora-tion and teamwork. Cooperative learning methods assume heterogeneity and emphasize interactive learning opportunities. They are better designed to cope with the diverse needs of students and the requirements for success in an interdependent world. Cooperative learning is an important element of global education.

* * *

In Chapter 1, Lee Anderson documented the reasons we must develop a global perspective in our schools. In Chapter 2, Barbara Tye pointed out that global education is a social movement, and she discussed ways in which it is becoming imbedded in the "deep structure of schooling."

Despite the inevitability of global interdependence and even though there is growing recognition of the need to develop a citizenry educated in the newer realities of our world, it will not be easy to bring a global perspective to the curriculum of our schools. It is not easy to change the deep structure, which is governed by tradition and deeply held beliefs; and as Steve Lamy pointed out in Chapter 3, there are forces in this country opposed to global education.

Even so, there is hope. Many states have mandated global studies. Those mandates have not had a marked impact yet at the school level, but they add legitimacy to the movement. It is at the school level where real reform will have to take place. If teachers are given time to reflect and plan together, change will occur.

There are curriculum programs in existence to which teachers may turn if they wish to bring a global perspective to their current classes or to which schools may turn if they wish to install new courses. Such programs exist in many disciplines; some are indisciplinary, some are thematic, and most are in the social studies. Of particular note are developments in history, geography, and economics.

Educational leaders, such as ASCD members, need to become familiar with these programs; they need to see the relationship between the changing world and curriculum development. We cannot rely on curriculum frameworks conceived 60-80 years ago. The future is here, and our children and youth should be prepared to live in it.

References

Agency for Instructional Technology. (1988). *Global Geography*. (Videotapes). Blooming-ton, Ind.: Agency for Instructional Technology.

Alger, C. (July 24, 1987). "Linking Town, Countryside and Legislature to the World." Address at a symposium on Oklahoma's International Future, Chamber of House of Representatives, Oklahoma City, Oklahoma. Columbus: Mershon Center, Ohio State University.

Association of American Geographers and the National Council for Geographic Educa-tion. (1984). *Guidelines for Geographic Education: Elementary and Secondary Schools*. Washington, D.C.: Association of American Geographers, National Council for Geographic Education.

Backler. A. (1986). *The Nature of Geographic Literacy*. (ERIC Digest ED 277 601). Bloomington, Ind.: Agency for Instructional Technology.

Backler, A., and R. Hanvey. (1986). *Global Geography*. New York: Teachers College Press, Columbia University.

Backler, A., and J. Stoltman. (1988). *A Teacher's Guide to Global Geography*. Bloomington, Ind.: Agency for Instructional Technology.

Brown, L. (1987). "Foreword." In *State of the World*, edited by Worldwatch Institute. New York: W.W. Norton.

Center for Innovative Diplomacy. (Winter 1988-89). "International Trade, Cultural Exchange, and Global Politics." *Bulletin of Municipal Foreign Policy* 3, 1.

College Entrance Examination Board. (1986). "World History, Geography, and Cul-tures." In *Academic Preparation in Social Studies. Teaching for Transition from High School to College*. New York: College Entrance Examination Board.

Council of Chief State School Officers. (1985). *International Dimensions of Education: Position Paper and Recommendations for Action*. Washington, D.C.: Council of Chief State School Officers.

Council of Europe. (1989). *FORUM* (A Quarterly Publication). Directorate of Press Information, Council of Europe, 67006 Strasbourg, Cedex, France.

Cox, A. (February 26, 1989). *The New York Times*.

Cutler, L.N. (1978). *Global Interdependence and the Multinational Firm* (Headline Series No. 239). New York: Foreign Policy Association.

Europe Today: An Atlas of Reproducible Pages. (1985). Wellesley, Mass.: World Eagle, Inc.

Foreign Policy Association. (1988). *U.S. Trade and Global Markets: Risks and Opportunities* (Topic 3 in Great Decisions Series). New York: Foreign Policy Association.

Graves, N., O.J. Dunlap, and J. Torney-Purta, eds. (1984). *Teaching for International Understanding, Peace and Human Rights*. Paris: UNESCO.

Gross, R.E. (May 1977). "The Status of the Social Studies in the Public Schools of the United States: Facts and Impressions of a National Survey." *Social Education* 41: 194-200, 205.

Hanvey, R. (1977). *An Attainable Global Perspective*. New York: The American Forum for Global Education.

Jarolimek, J., et al. (November-December 1977). "The Status of Social Studies Education: Six Case Studies." *Social Education* 41: 574-601.

Joint Council on Economic Education. (1980). *Strategies for Teaching Economics: World Studies*. New York: Joint Council on Economic Education.

Joint Council on Economic Education. (1988). *Teaching Strategies: International Trade (Secondary)*. New York: Joint Council on Economic Education.

Kennedy, P. (1987). *The Rise and Fall of the Great Powers: Economic Change and Military Conflict from 1500 to 2000*. New York: Random House.

Kennedy, P. (February 21, 1988). "Learning from History: Do Our Politicians Understand the Need?" *Courier Journal* (Louisville, Ky.).

Kniep, W.M. (1986). "Defining a Global Education by Its Content." *Social Education* 50: 437-446.

Kniep, W.M., ed. (1987). *Next Steps in Global Education: A Handbook for Curriculum Development*. New York: The American Forum.

McNeill, W. (1973). *The Ecumene: Story of Humanity*. New York: Harper and Row.

McNeill, W. (1979). *A World History*. London: Oxford University Press.

Mehlinger, H., ed. (1981). *UNESCO Handbook for the Teaching of Social Studies*. Paris: UNESCO.

Mehlinger, H., and J. Tucker, eds. (1979). *Teaching Social Studies in Other Nations* (Bulletin No. 60). Washington D.C.: National Council for the Social Studies.

Mershon Center. (1976). *Columbus in the World: The World in Columbus*. Columbus: Mershon Center, Ohio State University.

Mershon Center (1987). *American History and National Security*. Columbus: Mershon Center, Ohio State University.

Ministry of Education of Japan. (n.d.). *The American Revolution: Selections from Secondary School History Books of Other Nations; As Others See Us; Education for International Understanding: The United States as a Case Study; Verdict on America*. Tokyo: Ministry of Education of Japan.

Morrissett, I. (April-May 1986). "Status of Social Studies: The Mid-1980's." *Social Education* 50: 303-310.

National Commission on Social Studies in the Schools. (1989). *Charting a Course: Social Studies for the 21st Century*. Report of a joint project of the American Historical Association, Carnegie Foundation for the Advancement of Teaching, National Council for the Social Studies, and the Organization of American Historians. Washington, D.C.: National Commission on Social Studies in Schools.

National Council for the Social Studies. (January 1984). "The World Economy: An Overview." *Social Education* (Special Issue). Washington, D.C.: National Council for the Social Studies.

National Geographic Society. (1986). *Maps, the Landscape, and Fundamental Themes in Geography*. (Map Poster). Washington, D.C.: National Geographic Society.

Ravitch, D. (1989). "International Studies in the California Framework." In *Access* (No. 86-87). New York: The American Forum for Global Education.

Reischauer, E.O. (May 29, 1976). "Expanding the Limits of History." *Saturday Review*, p. 20.

Remy, R.C., and R. Woyach. (1983). "The Local Communities in International Education: Assessing Needs and Opportunities." *Mershon Center Quarterly Report* (Ohio State University) 8, 2.

Shaver, J.P.; O.L. Davis, Jr.; and S.W. Helburn. (February 1979). "The Status of the Social Studies: Impressions from Three NSF Studies." *Social Education* 43: 150-153.

Social Studies Development Center. (1982). *Parallel Passages: Contrasting Views from Japan and the United States*. Bloomington, Ind.: Social Studies Development Center, Indiana University.

Stavrianos, L. (1964). "A Global Perspective in the Organization of World HIstory." In *New Perspectives on World History* (34th Yearbook of the National Council for the Social Studies). Washington, D.C.: National Council for the Social Studies.

Stavrianos, L.S. (1979). *A Global History*. Boston: Allyn and Bacon.

Study Commission on Global Education. (1987). *United States Prepares for Its Future*. New York: Global Perspectives in Education.

Switzer, K.A., and P.T. Mulloy. (1987). *Global Issues: Activities and Resources for the High School Teacher*. Boulder, Colo.: Social Science Education Consortium.

Thompson, J.M., and K. Hedberg. (1977). *People and Civilization: A World History*. Boston: Ginn and Company.

Von Laue, T.H. (November 1981). "What History for the Year 2000?" *The History Teacher* 15, 1.

Weitzman, D., and R. Gross. (1977). *The Human Experience*. Boston: Houghton Mifflin.

The World Bank. (1981). *Toward a Better World: A Case Study of Economic Development* (Multimedia Kit). Washington, D.C.: The World Bank.

The World Bank. (1988). *The Development Data Book*. Washington, D.C.: The World Bank.

The World Bank. (1989). *GNP Per Capita* (Poster Kit No. 3 in Measures of Progress Series). Washington, D.C.: The World Bank.

The World Economy and the Multinational Corporation. (1984). Peoria, Ill.: Caterpillar.

Worldwatch Institute. (1989). *State of the World* (A Report of Progress toward a Sustainable Society). New York: W.W. Norton.

Woyach, R., and R.C. Remy. (1988). *Approaches to World Studies: A Handbook for Curriculum Planners*. Needham Heights, Mass.: Allyn and Bacon.

State and Local Guidelines

California State Department of Education. (1985). *Model Curriculum Standards: Grades Nine through Twelve.* Sacramento: California Department of Education.

California State Department of Education. (1987). *History-Social Science Framework.* Sacramento: California Department of Education.

Center for Human Interdependence (CHI). (1988). *Orange County in the World.* Orange, Calif.: CHI, Chapman College.

Illinois State Board of Education. (1988). *Increasing International and Intercultural Competence through the Social Sciences.* Springfield: Illinois Board of Education.

Iowa Department of Education. (1989). *A Guide for Integrating Global Education Across the Curriculum.* Des Moines: State of Iowa Department of Education.

Massachusetts State Department of Education. (1985). *Massachusetts in the World.* Boston: Massachusetts Department of Education.

Mershon Center. (1976). *Columbus in the World.* Columbus: Mershon Center, Ohio State University.

Mershon Center. (1987). *American History and National Security.* Columbus: Mershon Center, Ohio State University.

Missouri Department of Elementary and Secondary Education. (1986). *Missouri in the World.* Jefferson City: Missouri Department of Elementary and Secondary Education.

New York State Assembly. (1988). (A proposed act to amend the education law, in relation to education for international communication and American economic competitiveness.)

New York State Department of Education. (1983). *Education for a Global Perspective: A Plan for New York State.* Albany: New York State Department of Education.

Wisconsin Department of Public Instruction. (1986). *Global Studies in Wisconsin Schools: Definitions and Directives.* Madison: Wisconsin Department of Public Instruction.

5

School Leadership and Global Education

Jane A. Boston

Teacher A was bright and enthusiastic. She had been assigned to teach the 6th grade class next to mine in 1982. It was her first year at this grade level, and we soon began to collaborate regularly. One of my own strong interests was the district's global education project. I was a member of a districtwide team responsible for developing a resource bank of materials and staff development activities for our colleagues. An opportunity arose to form a site team at our school. Teacher A, along with a few others, agreed to make up that team and participate in a team-building workshop sponsored by the regional project that supported our school district's efforts. All went well until the second session of the workshop, when we were asked to report on our small-group brainstorming session. I encouraged Teacher A to represent our group. With some reluctance, she did so, but later openly shared her discomfort and her anger at me for setting up the situation. She stressed that she preferred to stay in the background and did not want to be a leader.

Today Teacher A is completing her administrative credential. Over the past several years, she has served as the team leader for the districtwide global education team, teacher associate for the regional project, and staff member for two intensive summer institutes at a large university. She is a widely respected workshop leader. This transformation, and many others that I've had the opportunity to observe over the past ten years, continue to interest me. What factors contribute to the development of leadership? Does the content or structure of global education play any role in such development? Why does it happen for some and not for others? What roles do teacher leaders play in the relative success of new programs? What new issues arise for teachers as a result of their emerging leadership?

Other questions concern the role of principals and other administrators. Principal A met regularly with project staff from the Center for Human Interdependence (CHI). He voiced strong support for the CHI global education program and offered access to the faculty. He arranged for meetings and made sure all logistics were handled with great care. He stopped in to see that things were going well whenever the CHI staff worked with the teachers. At the end of three years, however, the global education program in the school was still struggling; initial interest from the teachers seemed to be waning.

Principal B voiced strong support for building a global perspective into the curriculum of the school. He consulted with the faculty and then warmly welcomed CHI's offer to support their efforts. The staff held "interest meetings," and CHI was invited to participate in them. Principal B joined with the staff in the meetings and participated actively in planning for use of CHI's resources. Three years later, Principal B had left the school—but the global education program was thriving. How do beliefs and behaviors of principals contribute to such different results? What interconnections exist between the culture of each school, its formal leadership, and the implementation of new programs? How do principals define and use leadership? What is the role of an outside agency such as CHI in influencing leadership in the school?

Throughout the United States, there is an emerging awareness of the need for an education that reflects the world's diversity, interdependence, and conflict and sets a broader context for effective U.S. citizenship. In response to this awareness, a number of global K-12 education programs are underway. Frequently, these efforts grow out of initiatives taken by colleges, universities, and world affairs organizations rather than the school district. (See Chapter 7, in which Jan Tucker discusses school and university partnerships.) School districts become willing partners in such change efforts, but are rarely the initial organizers. When global education becomes institutionalized into a school's curriculum, there has been a transfer of ownership from the initial outside organizer to both the formal and informal leadership of the school. The nature of leadership—that of the outside agency and that within the school—greatly influences how, and even if, that transfer is achieved.

Transfer of Vision and Leadership

It has become a truism that effective leaders hold clear visions for their organizations and have skills to actualize those visions. Underlying each vision is a clear rationale for why things need to be different and some strategies for closing the gap between what exists and what might be. A key task for an outside organizer of global education efforts is to help school leaders clarify their own vision. Once that vision is clarified and strategies are identified, outside resources and support systems can be used more effectively to help achieve the school's goals. The outsider can be facilitator, coach, and information source; but he cannot carry the vision for the school or exercise leadership within it.

Who then must carry the initial vision to focus a school's change efforts? It may be a key district administrator (superintendent, curriculum coordinator), a site principal, a teacher leader, or a community member (usually a board member). The degree to which that individual holds a clear vision, has the requisite skills to share and actualize it, and understands her own school's culture (including the larger context of the school district and community), the greater the chance a strong global education program will be established. It is my suspicion that Principal A never held such a vision. If he did, he may have lacked the leadership skills needed to engage others in working toward the vision. Alternatively, forces within the school culture that worked against such change may have been so pervasive that no one could alter their effects.

I'd like to focus more closely on two sources of initial school leadership in promoting global education: the principal and the teacher leader. Each has great power to bring change, and the ability of each to do so is highly dependent on the other and the school's total culture. Schein (1985) emphasizes the inseparable relationship between leadership and culture and suggests that the creation and management of culture may be a leader's most important task.

Principal's Role

Much has been written about the key role of the principal in supporting school-site change. Nothing in my experience contradicts that notion. Indeed, I cannot think of a single, strong school-site program in global education that has not enjoyed the support of its principal. Conversely, I can tell too many stories of frustrated teachers demoralized by a perceived lack of support after countless hours of effort that have resulted in little, if any, progress toward a curriculum that includes a global perspective. The principal has the power to facilitate or block change efforts. The messages he sends formally and informally about what is important have profound effects on the school's culture, climate, programs, and people. As Sergiovanni (1987) and others have pointed out, the ability of leaders to communicate their values and beliefs to others in a way that provides context and meaning is highly significant in the life of a school.

Principal B held a vision of global education for the students in the school. He demonstrated basic respect for those who would have to bring about such a change. He involved the teachers with him in the initial decision to participate in CHI's global education program. Once that decision had been made, he actively participated with the faculty in planning how to take best advantage of the CHI resource. The teachers in School B viewed themselves as active participants in shaping the school and as resources as well as learners in the project. All of the principal's behaviors were consistent with that view and his own belief that leadership is something to be spread and shared. Changes in the classroom were evident early in the project's life. Both principal and teachers demonstrated pride in their accomplishments. When Principal B left the school during the second year of the project, the program continued its momentum. He clearly had passed on to others the importance and meaning he ascribed to global education in the school.

Principal as Enabler. Several beliefs and behaviors seem to be common to principals in schools where effective global education programs exist. These principals take the following actions:

• Communicate the importance of a global education and articulate its rationale in ways that create shared meaning with others in the school.

• Demonstrate trust in the ability of teachers to make professionally responsible decisions about curriculum and their own professional development.

• Participate actively with the staff on matters of importance (e.g., setting goals for a global education program).

• Organize school resources and structures so that they support and facilitate work toward agreed-on goals (e.g., use of faculty meeting time, discretionary budget, scheduling that allows for collaborative planning and peer coaching).

• Identify outside resources that support work toward the school's goals and facilitate their use.

• Provide information that increases the staff's ability to mediate and integrate the multiple demands on their time, attention, and resources, allowing continued focus on shared goals.

• Encourage and facilitate the leadership of others.

• Support a school culture that acknowledges the need for recognition, risk taking, and regular reflection.

This list can be linked in many ways to countless other lists suggesting elements that contribute to improved school cultures and recommendations for restructuring decision-making relationships. Nevertheless, it is clear to me that where these beliefs and behaviors are present, it is more likely that a global education program will succeed.

Principal as Blocker. What happens when principals exhibit characteristics other than enabling behaviors? What are some alternative behavior patterns? Principal A seems to exemplify many of those whose actions block or at least inhibit the continuation of global education projects. At first glance, he appeared interested in bringing global education to the school. He gave verbal support to the idea and provided access to the staff at the school. He was cooperative in making logistical arrangements for meetings and other activities. He was an authoritative leader, making the decision to involve the school in

CHI's global education program, setting the times for extra meetings, identifying existing priorities to which the program should be tied, and determining who should participate in ongoing workshops. On the other hand, a rotational system that allowed teachers to take turns participating prevented consistent participation by any one teacher. And although Principal A visited meetings in which goals and activities for the global education program were being discussed, he did not actively participate. His apparent support for the project seemed to contradict what was happening with the faculty.

Moreover, informal leadership structures in the school seemed powerful and sometimes divisive. Faculty meetings were characterized by teacher behaviors that could be interpreted as a lack of respect for the principal's leadership. Morale was not high in the school, and teachers sometimes saw themselves as "victims." Some teachers using CHI's resources perceived little support for their work. I could not find evidence that shared meaning and purpose had been developed in the school around the global education theme. Principal A may appear different from principals who actively oppose global education as a priority in their schools or who give verbal commitment to a project, but do nothing at all to follow up—but the net results are the same. The program does not move forward with any significance.

Some general characteristics identify principals in schools where global education programs fail to take hold:

• They use a centralized leadership model with little formal involvement of teachers in goal setting and decision making. There is little evidence of shared goals.

• They give verbal support for programs but are not actively involved in ways that demonstrate to the faculty the importance of the program.

• They do little to facilitate teachers' use of resources and time in working toward goals.

• They are unable to clearly articulate a vision of a school with a global perspective and communicate its rationale.

• They make little attempt to facilitate integration among various program elements and resources.

• They focus on logistical management of programs rather than their design, content, and follow-up.

• They give little attention to rewarding teachers and actively developing the school culture.

• They are not perceived as learners who are interested in acquiring and integrating new knowledge into their own practice.

• They do not reflect much on ongoing programs.

• They depend on others—co-administrators, department heads, or teacher "volunteers"—to carry the global education program.

Generalizations are difficult to draw from this list. Are these principals creating or responding to the culture of their schools? Do they perceive global education as an underlying threat to the centralized management structure with which they are comfortable, in that the content of global education values the individual and encourages the exploration of multiple perspectives? Are they simply not interested in curriculum change of any nature? Are they managers rather than instructional leaders? I certainly cannot answer these questions. I can only observe that where some combination of these beliefs and behaviors dominate, attempts to implement global education are not successful.

Questions also abound concerning the relationship between culture and leadership. Do leadership characteristics arise from the culture of the school, or do they determine it? To what degree and at what rate is change in culture possible? Should the principal business of leaders be creating and managing the culture of the school, as Schein (1985) suggests? Is successful leadership unique to individuals, heavily dependent on the personality, developmental stage, knowledge, skills, and value structures of the individual principal? Are the patterns I have described unique to global education, or can they be generalized to planned change in other areas? Do these characteristics suggest that only one style of leadership can promote and sustain change within the school? Is that style limited to a subset of all principals? What does it tell us about the chances for integrating a global perspective into the majority of our nation's schools?

The Principal and Global Education. An elementary school principal who had recently been assigned to a school with a strong global education program told me that she had gone to the school full of ideas about developing shared leadership and collaborative planning. Her hopes were high for creating an excellent school, one in which students, teachers, and community interacted in a respectful and productive way. But, she said, when she arrived she found that what she dreamed about already existed. When I explored this further, she very clearly identified the school's global education team and the results of its work as the major factor in bringing the school community together around a clear vision of an education that included a global perspective.

In the school where this principal found herself, a global education team initiated by a single teacher four years before and supported by the principal had strengthened communication across grade levels, facilitated faculty sharing and the development of cross-age projects, published a monthly newsletter for teachers, raised outside resources to support shared goals, established schoolwide traditions, involved the community, and gradually engaged actively and positively all but one teacher.

Principals in schools with strong global education programs often link the content and assumptions of such a program to their larger vision of a "good" school. These principals believe that global education directly contributes to a more active awareness of the ongoing formation of the school's culture and the many cultures represented by both students and teachers. Moreover, exploring the concept of multiple perspectives develops critical thinking and can lead to richer, more respectful discussion of issues by both students and faculty. Both teachers and students benefit from a study of conflict management; they develop skills that can be applied to parent/teacher disagreements, playground fights, and staff disputes. The exploration of interdependent systems helps develop a wider appreciation for the mutual dependencies and complex interactions in the school, district, and community. The collaborative nature of many global education projects helps establish and reinforce norms of professional interaction and sharing. The interdisciplinary nature of global education content can help unify traditionally fragmented departments, grade levels, and programs around a common purpose.

Global education programs may also set up dynamics that challenge assumptions guiding more centralized, "top-down" decision making. Universally, global education projects highly regard teachers as professionals and treat them as key agents in effecting change. Teacher leadership is actively promoted and facilitated in projects throughout the country. Unless there is a clear, shared goal between the school's formal leadership and the global education project, the development of such leadership can lead to frustration and burnout by teachers when they encounter lack of acceptance of their ideas or passive resistance to the initiatives.

In one statewide project with which I work, a team of four teachers participated with several other teams in a two-week summer institute. The members of each team had been selected and endorsed by their school's administration. A major goal of the institute was for each team to develop goals and an action plan for beginning a global education project in their respective districts the following year. After a week and a half, the team developed an ambitious plan and enthusiastically went to share their ideas with their school's chief administrator. His reaction was swift: Teachers had no authority to make such plans; the plans themselves were inconsistent with the school's authority structure; and professional development plans suggested in the plan had no precedent in the school's history and were unacceptable. The administrator gave the team an "assignment" that was consistent with his goals for the school. The team returned to the institute demoralized and proceeded to complete their "assignment" with little enthusiasm. The last I heard, three of the four team members were hoping to leave the school and find other positions. All expressed a desire to be more involved in collaborative decision making and active professional development. Clearly the leadership development goals of the project were not well understood by the school's administrator when he agreed to participate in the program and send a team to the institute.

The Role and Development of Teacher Leadership

Teachers are providing much of the leadership in global education in the United States. They are participating as learners, improving their own knowledge and skills. They are working as members of teams and committees planning and providing staff development opportunities and resources to their colleagues. They are rewriting district curriculum guidelines and developing new curriculum materials. They are changing their own classroom practices and supporting others who are engaged in similar change. They are learning to understand the cultures of their schools and to apply that understanding in working with administrators and community members in planned change processes.

Those recommending teacher "empowerment" and restructuring of decision making in schools can find evidence to support their proposals in the contributions teachers are making to global education. Who are these teachers? What conditions have allowed their leadership to flourish? What issues arise for these teachers?

Teachers participating in global education projects seem to represent a broad spectrum. Many are seasoned teachers, nearing the end of their careers; others have less than five years' experience. Some are teachers who quickly engage in every new curriculum trend that comes along; others may have been labeled "burned out" by their administrators and colleagues. Some regularly participate as teacher leaders and mentors in their districts; others are not involved in any other activity outside their own classrooms. Some are powerful "gatekeepers" in their own schools. Some are widely traveled; others have never been outside their own state. They represent the entire K-12 range.

Let's explore in more depth the story of Teacher A, the teacher in the opening vignette of this chapter, to see what may have stimulated the changes in self-perception from someone who wanted to remain in the background to someone who now takes formal leadership roles in highly visible settings. The program in which she participated was sponsored by the Bay Area Global Education Program, currently one of the nine resource centers of the California International Studies Project. Her first exposure to global education had come through faculty meetings at our elementary school and through personal interaction with me. There were no demands on her to participate. Resources and professional development opportunities were available; but she controlled the decision of how, when, or whether to use them. Entry into the project was available at many levels of involvement, ranging from using curriculum materials to participating actively on a team responsible for school site planning and program development.

Teacher A first chose to use materials made available by the project and to attend some districtwide awareness workshops. After some time, she joined the school site team and enrolled in a two-week summer institute on Africa at Stanford University. A districtwide global education project provided a context in which teachers were viewed as resources; and when Teacher A returned from the Africa institute, she was seen as a resource for others and was invited to share what she'd learned in a districtwide workshop. To allay her fears about presenting for the first time, she was paired with another teacher who had more workshop experience. The summer institute provided her with models of other teachers doing curriculum presentations and with an abundance of curriculum material. For the next several years, the project continued to offer additional opportunities for Teacher A to share her professional talents and try out new behaviors in a supportive environment.

A number of factors were present in the situation that nourished Teacher A's considerable talents:

- Although the project was formally supported by both the district and the school, the nature and intensity of involvement was left to the professional judgment of the teacher.

- Many opportunities were available for her to explore roles outside the classroom that acknowledged her competency and increased the opportunity for her to interact regularly with colleagues.

- Team structures at both the school site and district levels provided focus and support as she selected and tried new behaviors in and outside of the classroom.

- The school's principal believed in the value of the program, and he demonstrated his support by allocating time and resources.

- Regional project meetings allowed Teacher A (1) to see many other teachers modeling global curriculums; (2) to participate in collaborative program planning, implementation, and assessment; and (3) to participate in team-building activities.

- She had regular access to a resource library and content-based workshops, institutes, and study tours.

- Underlying it all was a basic respect for her as a professional and sufficient reward structures to sustain her motivation.

Sprinthall and Thies-Sprinthall (1983) have identified elements that compose a model for adult learning: (1) significant role-taking experiences, (2) careful and continuous guided reflection and integration, (3) continuous programs, and (4) personal support and challenge.

Many global education projects, sometimes without explicit recognition of the links to adult development, have structured these elements into their programs. I suspect that this structure has contributed considerably to the development of leaders like Teacher A.

Teacher B was known as a master teacher in his high school. When applications for mentorship were distributed, he decided to pursue his personal interest in global education and apply. As a former administrator, his planning and organizational skills were well developed, and he was respected by fellow teachers. The mentorship was approved, and he proceeded to implement his plans to share resources with fellow teachers. Teacher B carefully researched available curriculum materials and learning opportunities and prepared a bimonthly newsletter that he distributed to fellow teachers. He followed up and provided specific materials for teachers who requested information on particular programs or topics. He took materials from the district's resource bank to each high school and spent time in the library during teachers' break time to make the materials easily accessible. Invitations to join Teacher B on a team to run the project received no response. Near the end of the year, Teacher B arranged for a speaker of national renown to do a workshop for the district. Personal invitations were issued to each teacher and administrator, with reminders placed in each person's mailbox the day of the workshop. The home economics department of one of the high schools prepared elaborate desserts, and a local business park donated space for the workshop. The evening of the workshop arrived. Five teachers out of a total faculty of more than 150 attended, three of whom came from his own school. No district or site administrator attended. When the year ended, Teacher B was encouraged to renew his mentorship application for the following year. He declined—and, to date, no work on global education has gone forward in the district.

A number of factors influenced the fate of Teacher B's project. Although the mentorship was formally endorsed by the district, there was no clearly held vision for global education either in the district or at any school site. There was no active support from any district or school site administrator. Teacher B had no support system either in the district or outside. The new mentor program was viewed with skepticism by most teachers. There was no opportunity for collegial interaction in planning, implementing, or evaluating phases of the project. The district's culture had little precedent for voluntary staff development at the high school level. Staff morale was strained due to labor/management difficulties. In sum, there was no legitimacy for the project and no deep support in the district's culture.

Teacher B's knowledge, skill, and willingness to share could have provided the initial energy for a strong program in many other settings. His experience highlights the critical interdependence among formal leadership, informal leadership, and school culture. We cannot understand and interpret one without also examining the others.

Most teachers receive their initial introduction to global education at an awareness workshop or faculty meeting. It is common for a few teachers to immediately gravitate to the ideas and resources presented. This first group of teachers may exercise considerable influence over whether the project takes hold in their school. Assuming the culture supports renewal and change, teachers who are respected by their colleagues can provide legitimacy to a new program very quickly. Teacher B had the respect of his colleagues but was working in a culture that did not support professional development.

If initial interest is centered with teachers who are outside the mainstream faculty culture, the spread of a project may be seriously impaired. Establishment of shared goals for global education can be held hostage by interdepartmental rivalries or teacher cliques. Bright, energetic teachers sometimes carry a program for a while through personal energy and charisma. If they leave or lose interest, the program dies. Sometimes leadership teams become private clubs, with the "leadership group" unconsciously closing out the participation of others in the project.

Teacher leaders in schools with strong global education programs exhibit many of the same characteristics as their principals. They hold a clear vision of global education in their schools and understand its rationale. They are able to communicate their beliefs to others and are not afraid to share leadership. They exhibit basic respect for their colleagues and welcome collaborative work. They see themselves as active learners and seek new information regularly.

The emergence of teacher leadership in global education seems to follow a general pattern. There is first a general awareness of the need for doing something more to prepare students for the changing nature of the world. This is followed by an exploration and testing of some existing curriculum resources in the classroom. These efforts are usually modest and sporadic. Through ongoing interaction with others, the teacher begins to form a clearer vision of global education. New questions and additional needs for professional development emerge. Norms for collegial support are internalized and result in more risk taking in the classroom and with colleagues. Over the course of three to five years, the teacher's own classroom moves toward full infusion of a global perspective. Participation in teams and other global education project activities allows the teacher to share what she is learning with others and to refine her own practice as a result. The teacher's sense of efficacy increases and is recognized by others. Lieberman and Miller's (1984, 94) suggested list of conditions for improvement—"participation, continued support, rewards and resources, and the excitement of becoming more competent"—all seem present for these teacher leaders.

What are the results of this increased pool of teacher leaders? The resource they represent is immense. They often become the foundation for implementing other district programs and curriculum plans. Many are called on by neighboring districts as resources in professional development activities or are appointed to state and professional association leadership roles.

This increased sense of professionalism and efficacy, however, leads to dissatisfaction with classroom roles for a number of experienced teachers. Some of the most competent teacher leaders express their desire to move on to positions in which they believe they will have greater opportunity to use their professional knowledge and skill. For others, there is great frustration that the school's traditional structures provide few outlets to exercise continued leadership and collegial interaction. A cycle of burnout seems to exist, particularly among teachers whose continued efforts have not received strong administrative support or clearly moved their school toward an effective global education program. Teachers who exhibit high initial commitment and energy may withdraw and express bitterness that their considerable investment of time and talent has not moved the program into a position that is formally supported by a deep district commitment and resources.

Outside agencies promoting global education and their partner school districts need to carefully consider not only the curriculum and the implications of such projects, but the impact of the resulting teacher leadership development. In a sense, each school-university partnership is a new institution, one that represents its member organizations, yet is different from them. If the goals and norms of the partnership are not closely aligned with those of the member organizations, teachers may get caught in confused role relationships. They may invest energy toward a vision that is not shared by their home institution. Certainly that was what happened to the team of teachers I described earlier. In some cases, teacher leadership may be strong enough or the culture of a school may be receptive enough that the visions eventually are integrated. In other cases, the gap becomes more pronounced with time.

Leadership, School Culture, and Global Education

More questions are raised than answered whenever one explores leadership. I have not discussed the infinite combinations of personality, developmental readiness, knowledge, skill, understanding, and culture that lead to unpredictable, illogical patterns of success and failure for global education programs. I have only alluded to the complex impact of the "deep structure" of schooling discussed by Barbara Tye in Chapter 2. An appreciation of this structure, as well as a better understanding of leadership, may help us build strong global education programs in every school in the nation. If global education is to become part of a school's program and culture, we must expand our current understanding of leadership and school culture, as follows:

• Principals must communicate to others their strong belief in the importance of global education and support that assertion by providing resources and time for teachers to design, implement, and assess curriculum and teaching practice, as well as upgrade their own knowledge and skills.

• Norms of the school culture must support change efforts, collegial interaction, and respect for teachers as professionals.

• Teacher leaders must share a strong vision of global education with others in their school and direct their change efforts toward that vision. They must recognize their own accountability to the larger context of their school, district, and community.

• Outside agencies supporting school change in global education must ensure that their efforts are built around a clear vision that is held by school leadership—principal and teachers. If such a vision does not exist, the agency should assist the school in developing and clarifying a vision before engaging in random program activities. The focus of an outside agency should always be on helping the school achieve the vision of its leadership. Initiative should clearly rest in the hands of those for whom the program must hold meaning if it is to succeed.

School administrators may want to reexamine global education to see how its underlying concepts and values not only improve children's understanding of the world, but may actively support other school goals. As a principal, I could not separate the benefits global education provided our instructional program from the support it lent to our efforts to improve playground relationships, our productive use of multiple perspectives in faculty discussions, or our efforts to integrate an increasing diversity of languages and cultural backgrounds into our school. The methods promoted in the project supported our efforts to improve critical thinking and increase interactive teaching. My own leadership skills and understanding of school culture were largely developed from personal experience as a teacher and a team leader responsible for building a global education program in my previous school and district. Perhaps most important, the program's concepts, processes, and opportunities supported professional growth for all staff members.

* * *

Those who are affiliated with colleges, universities, and world affairs organizations and who want to support schools' efforts in establishing global education programs need to more explicitly acknowledge and seek to understand the potential for making a broad impact on schools—beyond inclusion of global projects in the formal curriculum. Research on both global education and school change (e.g., the project undertaken by CHI) should help us better understand these dynamics. As our understanding of leadership, school culture, and global education increases, our effectiveness in preparing students for an interdependent, diverse, and changing world should also improve. The school itself is a microcosm of that larger world, providing us with perhaps an even stronger rationale for the inclusion of global education in the schools.

References

Lieberman, A., and L. Miller. (1984). *Teachers, Their World, and Their Work*. Alexandria, Va.: Association for Supervision and Curriculum Development.

Schein, E.H. (1985). *Organizational Culture and Leadership*. San Francisco: Jossey-Bass.

Sergiovanni, T.J. (1987). "The Theoretical Basis for Cultural Leadership." In *Leadership: Examining the Elusive. The 1987 ASCD Yearbook*. Alexandria, Va.: Association for Supervision and Curriculum Development.

Sprinthall, N.A., and L. Thies-Sprinthall. (1983). "The Teacher as an Adult Learner: A Cognitive-Developmental View." In *Staff Development: NSSE Yearbook*. Chicago: National Society for the Study of Education.

6

Teacher Development Through Global Education

Ida Urso

The world is at our doorstep, and we cannot help being aware of it. As a matter of fact, in the closing months of 1989, we have all watched the news in amazement as one barrier after another has fallen in Eastern Europe. In many respects, the world seems to be changing for the better: new technology has improved the conditions of life for many people, and the end of the Cold War has provided what seems to be an opportunity to abandon the senseless and dangerous arms race.

On the other hand, our world seems to be spinning out of control: world hunger and homelessness are ever present; there is global environmental degradation of life-threatening proportions; and we are witnessing a growing gap between the haves and the have-nots. Increasingly, teachers everywhere, and especially in the United States, are becoming aware of the need to prepare young people for a different kind of life—a life in which new conditions will require constructive adaptation, and new problems will require creative solutions.

In casting about for ways to adapt the elementary and secondary school curriculums to this new need, teachers are finding that global awareness education can provide them with the knowledge and the tools they need. They also find that becoming involved with global education yields some unanticipated rewards of a more personal nature: it has the potential to "recharge their batteries," to help them feel excited about teaching again.

Sources of Teacher Discouragement

It is certainly no secret that the circumstances of education in America, toward the close of the 20th century, are problematic. The information explosion since the end of World War II and changing societal conditions have combined to alter our expectations of schools. Far more than ever, Americans expect schools—and teachers—not only to educate children, but to socialize, raise, and train them as well. The resulting proliferation of the curriculum (adding new knowledge and skills to be taught, while rarely deleting anything) leaves teachers frustrated: "*How on earth can I do justice to everything they expect me to cover?*" We're speaking here not only of the regular subject matter taught in classes, but also of the other issues that teachers face: teenage pregnancy, AIDS awareness, signs of suicidal tendencies, and suspected cases of child abuse. In addition, teachers must help improve the self-esteem and confidence of young people, diffuse the attractions of gang membership, correctly diagnose and remediate learning disabilities, recognize cases of eating disorders, and appropriately counsel children who are distressed due to conditions at home or who are threatening to run away. We really expect our teachers to do it all.

Moreover, we expect teachers to do everything on a shoestring, with outdated equipment and inadequate supplies. We allow them no input into budget decisions, and we provide little or no training for their expanded roles. Then we pay them salaries that have actually declined, in real dollars, since the '70s. We don't allow them time to talk with each other, to solve their school problems, or to plan together; and we hardly ever say "thank you" or give them a public compliment. It's little wonder that many good teachers get discouraged and leave the profession, and that those who choose to remain are reluctant to get involved in anything other than their basic teaching duties. There simply isn't enough time or energy left.

Global Education: An Encouraging Force

From 1985 to 1989, teachers in 11 elementary and secondary schools in Orange County, California, were invited to participate in a global awareness education project sponsored by the Center for Human Interdependence (CHI) at Chapman College. Various components of the project are described elsewhere in this book; the focus of this chapter is the discovery by many teachers that participating in CHI activities helped them to feel a new excitement about their teaching. Related benefits included heightened student interest and motivation, as well as improved faculty morale.

We selected global awareness education as the substantive vehicle for our project for three major reasons: the promotion of cross-cultural understanding, the incorporation of holistic learning, and the potential for community involvement.

Cross-Cultural Understanding

Global education is meaningful and relevant, and it connects both teachers and students to new knowledge and perspectives. Global education deals with critical current issues that are in daily newspaper headlines and that form the lead stories on nightly news broadcasts. Bringing such issues into the classroom provides a sense of immediacy and connects the classroom to the real world, making learning more relevant as well as more dynamic and interesting. (See Chapter 1 of this book, by Lee Anderson; see also Anderson 1968.)

This emphasis on current issues includes the promotion of cross-cultural awareness and understanding, an issue of special significance in southern California and other public schools, where "minority" students will soon outnumber Anglo students. In fact, the CHI teachers believed this aspect of global education was by far the most important.

Moreover, global education emphasizes the need to develop "perspective consciousness," which generally means that we can recognize the existence of more than one valid point of view, and that we learn to see the world from a number of different perspectives. This is a challenging but necessary skill when, increasingly throughout the United States, such a variety of cultures, races, and ethnic groups live side by side and when, through one crisis or another, the world is almost daily brought to our doorstep.

Global education becomes a dynamic, exciting presence in the classroom as it helps teachers and students connect with and make sense of the quickly changing world around us, as the following teacher comments illustrate:

> Global education raises the awareness for children that we all share the same planet, that there's more to the world than their neighborhood, and it helps dispel prejudices at a young age—a point of concern in Orange County because of the incoming immigrants.

> Global education helps my students become aware of and hopefully understand other cultures, countries, and people from a social, political, and economic point of view.

> Global education helps my students understand the "how" and the "why"—the cause-and-effect relationships between events around the world which affect their daily lives.

Holistic Learning

The second reason we chose global education as our focus is that it encourages holistic learning. Not only does it foster the integration of learning and therefore lend itself well to interdisciplinary teaching and learning experiences, but it also calls for the education of the whole student. Different proponents of global education call our attention to the holistic nature of global education. For example, Robert Muller (1977), Chancellor of the United Nations University for Peace in Costa Rica, refers to the need for learning that will address the "world of the heart" as well as the "world of the mind." Lee Anderson, one of the authors of this book, wrote in 1968 about the need for global education to "develop the capacity of students intellectually and emotionally to cope with continuous change." Shiman and Conrad (1977) have argued that awareness and action, as well as understanding, are needed. And Richard Berendzen (1988) called for educators to "touch the future" of global awareness (see also Johnson 1989, Mische 1987, Steele and Andrews 1988, and Urso 1985).

Real-life issues can best be taught from a holistic perspective, bringing the various disciplines to bear on one issue and incorporating many modalities of learning, such as simulations, role playing, experiential learning, and integration of the arts. Several CHI teachers chose this as a primary reason for becoming involved with global education. In the words of one teacher, "Global education is important because it provides a holistic approach, where children are educated not only in academics, but also as contributing members of our society, our country, and our world."

Community Involvement

The third reason we chose global education is its potential to involve the community. As Charlotte Anderson shows in Chapter 8, global education can bring about healthy and vital interactions between the community and the classroom. Many of the CHI teachers made good use of a resource directory published by CHI, which listed free or inexpensive resources in the community—groups, organizations, or individuals who would visit classrooms with the intent of broadening students' horizons in some appropriate way. Teachers also used the resource directory to find nearby sites for interesting and pertinent field trips.

CHI teachers also encouraged students to bring in parents, relatives, or friends to talk about their immigrant experiences, life in their native country, international work experiences, and so forth. Many parents and other community members also took part in preparing international feasts or in presenting ethnic art for the classroom or for school assemblies.

CHI's Teacher-Centered Strategy

Throughout the four years of the project, CHI staff members functioned as facilitators, providing resources and opportunities as teachers requested them. The staff spent a great deal of time in the 11 project schools—delivering materials; visiting classes; talking informally in the halls, lunchrooms, or teachers' lounges; and generally being as helpful as possible. CHI had no predesigned curriculum to promote; rather, decisions about what to work on were made by the teachers themselves, individually or in voluntary groups.

The CHI philosophy was—and is—that most teachers are professionals; they truly care about their work, their students, and the society of which they are a part (see Ainsworth 1989). Given the opportunity, the resources, and sometimes the encouragement, teachers will involve themselves in self-renewing activities that make classroom life more relevant and interesting for their students. We believe that since we trust teachers to be alone with our children behind closed doors, we certainly should be willing to listen to their ideas and opinions about how they can best do their jobs.

The effectiveness and significance of this philosophy, which was translated into the many services and programs offered to teachers, cannot be overemphasized. In fact, it was our teacher-centered strategy that, in many cases, attracted teachers to the CHI project in the first place. Once involved, they found personal and professional satisfaction in trying to infuse some global awareness into their teaching. During the first year or two, CHI staff members were told that some teachers at the participating schools were still "waiting for the hook." But eventually, one by one, many of those teachers came to us to express their surprise at—and gratitude for—a project that did not impose itself, but was available as a resource for those who were interested.

Teachers at each of the 11 schools were introduced to CHI at a faculty meeting early in the fall of 1985. At that time, they heard a brief presentation about the importance of global awareness and about the idea of infusing global perspectives into the curriculum, in all subjects and at all grade levels. They were told that if enough of them were interested, resources could be made available to them: curriculum materials and reference books; audiovisual materials; guest speakers; conferences and inservice workshops on topics of their choice; release time for team planning of global awareness learning activities; access to expert consultants and resource people; opportunities to meet and share with other teachers already involved in global education efforts; and small grants for curriculum development projects. The possibilities were limited only by the teachers' interests and creativity.

After a short question-and-answer period, the teachers discussed the CHI proposal among themselves and filled out an interest inventory consisting of the following questions:

1. Which ideas regarding global perspectives would you like to pursue with your students?

2. Please list ways in which CHI could help you teach these ideas to your students.

3. Please share some of the ways you are presently helping students to develop a better understanding of global issues and concepts.

4. Please identify some of the resources you have used which you think are especially helpful.

Thus began the dialogue between CHI and the teachers, and among the teachers themselves. The responses to these questionnaires determined whether the schools would become members of the CHI network. Thus, too, began the partnership between CHI and the interested teachers at four elementary, four intermediate, and three high schools. As the teachers had been told, the responses to the inventory questionnaires were used to better understand their needs and interests, so that resource materials could be purchased, curriculum ideas shared, and workshops planned.

Especially Popular Activities

Along with the focus on service, another strategy that met with great success was an emphasis on "networking." Teachers found the opportunity to meet and share with their colleagues at other schools to be one of the most enjoyable and beneficial parts of the project. On workshop evaluations, we often found the highest marks were given to the period of time allowed for teachers to meet in small groups with their peers from different schools, subject areas, and grade levels. Much comradery was established as teachers shared their educational hopes and concerns and their ideas and experiences about common problems and successful solutions. The substance of a particular workshop was sometimes of secondary importance to the interactions teachers shared among themselves.

The value our teachers placed on networking was one of the main reasons that the "International Sports Day" met with such resounding success among participating teachers and students. In this program, the physical education teachers from the four intermediate schools and the one K-8 school came to the CHI office and, with the help of project staff, made plans for teaching their 7th graders eight games from around the world that stressed cooperation instead of competition. A month or two later, the teachers at each school chose 25 boys and 25 girls to be bused to the Chapman College athletic field. There, for an entire day in late May in 1987 and again in 1988, 250 students from a variety of different cultures, ethnic groups, and social backgrounds came together to enjoy a day of international games. The program was planned and carried out by the physical education teachers.

Another popular and effective project was "Your Community and the World," which teaches students about the ways in which their community is connected to other parts of the world. This program was modeled after the original "Columbus in the World" project, first developed at Ohio State University in 1972. Release time was provided for a group of 15 teachers from the network schools to meet at the CHI office for one day every two months during the course of a year. The teachers planned a project and carried it out with their students at some point during the year. At the beginning of the year, the teachers shared their ideas, then their plans; as the year went on, they were able to report to their colleagues how their project had fared in the classroom, including problems encountered and solutions found.

On the final evaluation questionnaires, the participating teachers were asked to clarify how their project had helped their students gain a global perspective. In all cases, the teachers pointed to the new understanding attained by their students. One teacher wrote, "The projects that my students did helped them to understand each other better, and to really look into their own backgrounds." Another wrote, "I think global education, as taught through this project, is important. Only by understanding our similarities will we have peace in the world."

Another popular part of the CHI project was the minigrants offered to teachers who wanted to develop curriculum units that contained some global awareness activities or a global awareness theme. Because teachers were encouraged to form interdisciplinary teams and work together on projects across subject areas, a total of 142 teachers were awarded 65 small grants (totaling $43,926 and not exceeding $600 per teacher) over four years. Of all the proposals submitted, only a few were rejected. If a choice had to be made, because of yearly budget allocations, the preference was to award smaller amounts of money to a greater number of teachers, and to make awards to teachers who had not submitted proposals in previous years.

As can be imagined, grant applications increased yearly as teachers began to develop interest in global awareness and to trust the CHI process. Eighteen of the grants went to elementary school teachers, 29 to intermediate school teachers, and 17 to high school teachers. Reading the teachers' grant proposals provides some insight into their underlying view of what would be important to students at their level of schooling. At the elementary level, all but two of the projects focused on building an awareness and understanding of culture. The emphasis was on people from around the world—how they eat, live, and learn and how they entertain themselves through literature, music, dance, and art. One of the two projects that did not share this focus was about world geography and endangered animals; the other involved the purchase of a global data bank for the school library.

Twenty-three projects were designed to develop cross-cultural under-standing, the most popular theme at the intermediate schools. Three projects focused on environmental issues (environmental interdependence, the pro's and con's of using nuclear energy, and a study of the flora and fauna of the world); two dealt with increasing students' access to global data and information about global issues (one project chose to build a data base of facts and statistics on the nations of the world, and the other project chose to help mainstreamed special education students who were taught about global issues by focusing on globally related stories reported in the local newspaper). The third project dealt with global geography. This particular intermediate school has a huge world-map outline permanently painted on the concrete in the central area of the campus. It is used for many activities and serves as a constant reminder to all that being aware of the world we live in is now an educational imperative.

The 17 high school grant projects were more diversified. Nine dealt with cross-cultural understanding; the others focused on the recognition and documentation of interethnic and interracial tensions on the campus; environmental issues; global telecommunications; the creation of a data base in the school's guidance department on the international studies programs available in colleges and universities in the United States; the connections among various global problems such as population, hunger, and pollution; and the creation of interdisciplinary methodologies through which to teach global awareness.

New Directions for Teachers

Because it was important to the CHI staff that the project not be seen at any school as the "property" of one small group of interested people, we kept reaching out, in the third and fourth years, to involve teachers who had not yet participated. Ultimately, approximately half of the teachers in all of the schools were involved in one way or another. We consider this a significant achievement in light of the daily pressures, competing demands, and discouragements that teachers encounter.

What pleased us most, however, was the evidence that exposure to global awareness education was making a significant contribution to the vitality with which teachers approached their work. Teachers were experiencing new satisfaction when they incorporated global perspectives into their teaching. Early in the project, at one of the theme workshops, an English teacher remarked, "After 14 years of teaching, I feel rejuvenated!" Also, at one of the high schools, a social studies teacher and a science teacher became global education mentor teachers—a position of significant influence within that school district, involving a great deal of responsibility for providing inservice experience for other teachers. One of these, the science teacher, told us: "You've opened a new door for me, and I am so grateful."

References

Ainsworth, J. (Spring 1989). "Teachers' Higher Level Needs Unsatisfied." *Holistic Education Review* 2, 1: 33-37.

Anderson, L. (November 1968). "An Examination of the Structure and Objectives of International Education." *Social Education* 32, 7: 639-647.

Berendzen, R. (1988). *Touch the Future: An Agenda for Global Education in America*. Emmaus, Pa.: Rodale International.

Johnson, D. (Summer 1989). "Signs of a World Awakening: Consciousness, Values and Global Issues." *Noetic Sciences Review*, No. 11: 38-41.

Mische, P.M. (Spring/Summer 1987). "Educating for What? Human Learning and the Future of Peoples and Planet." *Breakthrough* 8, 3-4: 8-16.

Muller, R. (1977). Speech at the meeting of the New Group of World Servers Festivals Week, New York.

Shiman, D., and D. Conrad. (December 1977). "Awareness, Understanding, and Action: A Global Conscience in the Classroom." *The New Era* 58, 6: 163-167.

Steele, R.E., and M.P. Andrews. (January 1988). *Interconnections: Issues That Affect Local Communities and the World*. East Lansing: Michigan State University, Cooperative Extension Service.

Urso, I. (1985). "Worldmindedness: The Path to Peace and Justice." In *Global Images of Peace: Transforming the War System* (pp. 196-206), edited by T.M. Thomas, D.R. Conrad, and G.F. Langsman. Kottayam, India: Prakasam Publications.

7

Global Education Partnerships between Schools and Universities

Jan L. Tucker

> *If it ain't broke, you haven't looked hard enough.*
> Tom Peters, *Thriving on Chaos*

he conventional wisdom about education says that partnerships between schools and universities (and colleges) are bound to fail. The cultural gap is simply too great, and the rewards of success on both sides are too minimal. Research and our own experience tell us that this bit of folklore is rooted in considerable historical truth (Sarason 1982, K. Tye and B. Tye 1985). The record of university involvement in schools is dismal.

A larger critique sees the university as lagging in its obligations to play a more vigorous societal role. According to Botkin, Elmandjra, and Malitza (1979), writing for the Club of Rome, "The universities should be leading a campaign toward improving human capacities." These authors continue:

> Instead, the world's 40 million university students and five thousand universities are either held or holding back from playing a leading role for which they should be destined. Problems of selective participation, narrow specialization, chauvinism of academic disciplines, neglect of vital issues, "citadel" mentality

of many administrators, and preoccupation with selfish social advancement all limit the relevance of one of humanity's major resources (Botkin et al. 1979, 94-95).

Regarding school-university collaboration in the United States, however, "The times, they are a'changin'." Recently, there has been a renewed, widespread interest in establishing joint efforts—in using the accumulated experience and research base to increase the chances of their success (Goodlad 1988, Ward and Pascarelli 1987, 192-209). The reasons for this contemporary interest in school-university partnerships are manifold. They include the national school reform movement of the 1980s, the push for more and higher quality content in the school curriculum, criticisms of higher education's role in the training of teachers, and the potential for dwindling enrollments in higher education. Global education is also playing an increasingly important role.

As a matter of fact, education has been pushed to the top of the national policy agenda after languishing in the backwaters of public concern for some time. An increasing number of politicians and citizens are realizing that education has been seriously neglected and that the nation is paying a high price for this neglect—a fact that most educators have known for a long time. Education, like other institutions in the United States, has been held hostage to the Cold War during the 45 years since the end of World War II. Now that the world is shifting from these destructive priorities toward the fresh challenge of competing in an interdependent global economy, we are frustrated that many of our current allies, as well as neutral countries, are quick-stepping ahead and are not looking back.

Historically, as a nation rich in natural resources, we have neglected our human resources, taking it for granted that time and individual initiative were on our side. In this important matter we are quite unlike other industrialized nations, such as The Netherlands, Japan, and West Germany, who have learned they must trade to live and that trading successfully in today's sophisticated global markets depends on a globally educated citizenry. In the United States, this period of benign neglect of our human resources, a practice as old as our national origins and culture, is ending with shocking abruptness.

As a nation, we have finally realized that national renewal depends largely on the quality of our human resources; and improving education cannot be left to chance. To achieve national renewal, education has become a high priority, and we are struggling to find and allocate our increasingly scarce material resources to invest in these human goals. Consequently, partnerships between schools and universities, designed to make maximum use of our resources, are linked directly to the national priority of improving international education at all levels. These same global forces that have largely created the need for school reform and, in turn, for school-university partnerships, also provide the framework for building those partnerships. We call it global education.

Global Education Context
for School-University Partnerships

Is there anything distinctive, or even unique, about global education that serves the development of school-university partnerships? The answer is: distinctive—yes; unique—maybe. Experience indicates that global education is an ideal context for forging these partnerships. Because global education has recently become a national priority, it has acquired a level of visibility and urgency that will attract the resources necessary to accomplish the task. Although school and university partnerships are the major concerns in this chapter, educational collaborations must include other groups, including business and labor, foundations, and a broad coalition of community-based, non-governmental agencies.

The potential of global education to energize collaborative efforts in education is evidenced in many of the recent national reports that have elevated global education to the top of the nation's agenda. For example, the National Governors' Association (NGA 1989) offers a six-point agenda for national renewal:

[The United States must]
Discover new and emerging international markets for American products, to become again the Yankee traders we once were.
Bring an international perspective to our daily living—to understand foreign nations and the people beyond our borders... to learn the international language of business.
Expand our research, and use our technology, to create both new products and new processes to maintain America's competitive position.
Capitalize on the natural advantages of American manufacturers and regain competitiveness in our domestic markets.
Improve our highways, airports, airways, and ports so we can move our people across town and our products around the globe.
Invest in the health, education, and training of our children so they can live healthier and more productive lives.

To achieve these goals, the NGA adamantly stated that international education is to be required and must be accomplished:

We must make international education a priority in this country. . . . Just how important is it to our country? As important as economic prosperity, national security, and world stability. . . . *International education must be an integral part of the education of every student.* . . . Our task is. . . to develop a comprehensive statewide strategy for international education that reaches all agencies, all levels of education, and even into the private sector. *Critical to our success will be the involvement of a broad coalition—teachers, school administrators and board members, legislators, university presidents, college faculty, and the business community—in developing this comprehensive plan* [emphasis added].

That global education has become a national priority does not automatically mean that it ought to be established as a priority in the schools, let alone become the basis of building school-university partnerships. It is, however, a starting point. And global education has other important educational attributes that lend themselves well to the current climate of school reform.

Global education has a successful track record at the grass roots. There have been two decades of program development occurring at local sites around the nation. Lee Anderson (1979) has argued that global education, at least in its early stages, has been more like a grassroots, bottom-up social movement on the order of progressive education rather than a specific curriculum domain or reform. In the late 1970s, the U.S. Office of Education gave global education a major boost nationally by funding many global education projects under the authority of Section 603 (Citizen Education for Cultural Understanding), Title VI, of the now-defunct National Defense Education Act (NDEA). Unfortunately, these programs disappeared when the parent NDEA program itself was folded into the current Higher Education Act. However, Section 603 planted the seeds of future projects. More recently, in the 1980s, several educational philanthropic agencies, such as the Danforth, Exxon, Hewlett, and Rockefeller foundations, have funded global education development programs, in which collaboration between local schools and universities has been given high priority.

One of the school-university partnerships originally supported by Section 603 and more recently by the Danforth Foundation is the Global Education Leadership Training Program, described by Toni Fuss Kirkwood in Chapter 9. This is a collaborative effort between Florida International University (the State University of Florida at Miami) and the Dade County Public Schools. This program was noted in the NGA (1989) report on international education as an example of an existing, successful school-university collaboration established for the purpose of infusing global education into a school system. Other local and regional examples of school-university collaboratives for global education include:

- The Center for Human Interdependence (CHI) at Chapman College in Orange, California, works with schools in Orange County (also described elsewhere in this book).
- The Mid-America Program in Global Education at Indiana University has worked over many years with school districts in midwestern states.
- The California International Studies Project, initiated by Stanford University and funded by the state of California, has established nine school-university collaborative efforts statewide to foster international education.
- The Center for Teaching International Relations at the University of Denver is a longstanding effort by a university to work with the schools to improve the teaching of international content.

- The Mershon Center and the College of Education of the Ohio State University, in collaboration with other campus units, have worked extensively in linking the university with local efforts in global education in Columbus and throughout Ohio.

Other important grassroots global education efforts have been initiated through state leadership with strong university support. For several years, Oregon has required all high school graduates to take a course in global studies. New York now requires all students to take a two-year global studies course in grades 9 and 10. This course focuses on the world's major cultural areas and ties these together with activities and lessons on interdependence, culture, change, and 12 other overarching global concepts. The Minnesota Department of Education has initiated a request for state funding that would enable global education programs to be developed and delivered statewide. The state of Arkansas has developed a similar program. And the list continues, to include some type of global education activity in almost every state in the Union. Therefore, the NGA report builds on and strengthens what is already underway.

Global education has additional, intrinsic attributes that can contribute to the development of strong school-university partnerships. Being interdisciplinary by nature, global education offers a wide range of contacts and linkages between universities and schools. Almost every department in a university can make substantial contributions to a school in the area of global education. These contributions can range from providing a university speakers' bureau of international students to serving as a natural site where high school and college students can jointly plan and participate in international campus events, such as a model United Nations. The possibilities are virtually unlimited. The schools have equally significant contributions to make to universities. For example, classroom teachers trained in global education can be valuable mentors as experienced master teachers who supervise beginning teachers from the university during their field participation and student teaching experience. A global education partnership provides the bridge for these and other linking activities.

The interdisciplinary nature of global education gives it great resilience in the "turf" conflicts that often arise when something new appears on the education scene. Global education is not a zero-sum game, where more for you is less for me, and vice-versa. Rather, it represents an expanding continuum, where more for you is commonly more for all of us. Everyone can contribute to its growth, especially students, who bring their cognitive and affective "maps" of the world right into the classroom. Thus, much of the content of global education enters the classroom through students. Student beliefs, knowledge, and experiences are increasingly important aspects of global education as our classrooms become more international and multicultural. In Miami, for example, 30 percent of the students were born in another country, and it is commonplace for an individual high school to have students from more than 50 of the world's nations.

The egalitarian nature of global education also tends to break down the condescending wall of "expertise" that often impedes the relationship between universities and schools. Global education draws its strength from its grassroots character and requires the content of international education to be meshed with the needs of individual schools and districts. Although global education must draw on the expertise of scholarly investigation, its successful application requires an equally profound understanding of education and schools. Therefore, the university and school personnel enter a global education partnership equal before the challenge. Each can learn from the other.

Global education stands in sharp contrast to the "teacher proof" assumptions of the packaged curriculums developed in the United States during the 1960s and 1970s. The "new" mathematics, science, and social studies were generally developed apart from local school settings and without substantial involvement by classroom teachers, or even teacher educators. Change in local schools depended on a dissemination model that emphasized the export of scholarly knowledge from universities and development centers to local settings where teachers, pupils, and parents were largely "uninformed." The major emphasis of this period was on the development of up-to-date materials, not teacher education. Because teachers had very little sense of ownership or deep commitment at the local level, these curriculum projects were eventually shelved and failed to bring about the significant changes that had been anticipated.

By contrast, global education is most successful where educators, parents, and community leaders combine their human, financial, and political resources at the local level. Teachers, not textbooks, appear to be primary carriers of the global education culture. Thus, program development in global education represents a labor-intensive effort—a function well served by school-university partnerships with responsibility for a finite local area. The specificity of the context and the proximity of the participants tends to ensure a greater accountability than the more diffuse and distant relationships that have characterized many school reform efforts in the past. As more people understand the need and become productively involved in their own settings, global education achieves a potential for releasing local energies and resources for school change to a degree unknown in the era of the packaged curriculum (Tucker 1982).

Qualities of Successful Global Education Partnerships

It may be true, as a colleague recently chided, that establishing a successful school-university partnership is at least as difficult as developing a joint business venture with the Soviet Union. The prospect is just as exciting, however; and the potential payoff for all parties is just as promising as such a business venture. School-university partnerships are not recommended for those who only bet on a sure thing or those who must show a profit on the balance sheet in the first year or two. The bottom line of success for a school-university partnership is the creation of a long-term trust relationship; a reliable, high-quality product; and the development of a market share that satisfies both partners. These are the same principles of success that executives of American corporations are learning as they emerge from their domestic cocoons to compete in the international economic arena. These goals take thoughtful planning, sufficient time, and adequate resources.

Four principles are essential to the creation and maintenance of successful school-university partnerships in global education: (1) culture and leadership are important; (2) global education is for everyone; (3) a partnership must be mutually rewarding; and (4) a conceptual framework for global education is needed.

Culture and Leadership

Rudyard Kipling wrote the classic line "East is East, and West is West; and never the twain shall meet"; he also penned the lesser known "How can they know England who only England know?" His contrasting meanings represent the two sides of the culture coin. On the one hand, people tend to hold deep-seated beliefs about cultural differences among groups of people—to the point that they can never join together, regardless of the circumstances. The educational problem, however, is that you cannot really develop a profound self-knowledge without an understanding of others, especially their point of view toward you. By analogy, we can apply Kipling's insights to the problem of forging a school-university partnership in global education. It may be true that serious problems have existed in previous incarnations of such arrangements. But the needs of a new era dictate a closer relationship. Therefore, we really have no choice but to cooperate, to learn more about each other—and to learn more about ourselves in the process. Global reality has created this opportunity.

James Fallows (1989) discusses the need and the potential for the United States to renew itself along the lines of the open society that initially made us world leaders. Fallows defines culture as the "voluntary behavior of ordinary people" and goes on to state:

> In the long run, a society's strength depends on the way that ordinary people voluntarily behave. Ordinary people matter because there are so many of them. Voluntary behavior matters because it's too hard to supervise everyone all the time. . . . Successful societies—those which progress economically and politically and can control the terms on which they deal with the outside world—succeed because they have found ways to match individual self-interest to the collective good. The behavior that helps each person will, as a cumulative ethos, help the society as a whole (Fallows 1989, 13-14).

The ethical quality of global education—matching individual self-interest to the collective good, in turn stimulating participants to higher levels of voluntary action—makes it a powerful force in education today. The idea of global education energizes the "voluntary behavior of ordinary people," to use Fallows' term.

Teachers, administrators, professors, corporate heads, labor leaders, and others have come to share the realization that the United States faces a very different future and that we are ill prepared to deal with it. This common concern about the future of the nation overwhelms the traditional "and never the twain shall meet" mentality and our business-as-usual approach to education, creating a readiness for change. We are recognizing, as Kipling suggested, that we need to know more about others to better understand our own strengths and weaknesses as we assess our potential for meeting global challenges. As a shared vision, global education can help shape the culture of schools and of universities to meet this perceived national deficiency and can clear a path for the development of partnerships between the two institutions.

Sarason (1982), from data gathered in a recent period when the need for collaboration was not so apparent, identified the (stereo)typical cultural attitudes of university and school personnel about each other.

Views of schools from the university:

- Textbooks and curricula tend to be dull and out of date.
- Teachers are not well grounded in their subject matter.
- Teachers do not make the learning experience stimulating.
- Teaching is primarily a "pouring in" of knowledge.
- Teachers are too conforming, intellectually and personally.
- Teachers tend not to be as bright as those in other professions.
- Schools are too bureaucratic, stifling creativity.

Views of the university from the schools:

- College teachers have no training for teaching.
- The reward system has little to do with quality teaching.
- Most courses are dull and are offered in large classes.
- The university is not interested in the needs of students.
- College life is in the "ivory tower."
- The university is unrelenting in its resistance to change.
- Universities are bureaucratic and tend to discourage new ideas (Sarason 1982).

Global education partnerships hold the potential for breaking down these misconceptions and other barriers between the two cultures that have traditionally separated universities and schools.

A successful, continuing global education partnership between schools and universities requires the evolution of a new, composite culture. This developmental process involves restructuring attitudes and behaviors around a new perspective without diminishing the strengths of the separate cultures that characterize the schools and the university. Visionary leadership is required.

According to Schein (1988), the essence of leadership is the creation, maintenance, and renewal of a culture, whether one is referring to national politics, corporate development, or a school-university partnership. At each stage of evolution of the culture—group formation, group building, group work, and group maturity—leadership plays a vital role. As noted earlier, this leadership task is made easier by global education because many participants have come to a shared realization of the societal importance of the task and its open characteristics.

Developing a trust relationship is the first and most important goal of leadership. The task is to get the leaders in the partnership on both sides to view themselves as "us" rather than "them." As Fallows suggests, expanding the radius of trust is a key factor in harnessing the creative energies and expanding the voluntary efforts of ordinary people. Once trust is established, leaders need to get out of the way. "The United States has done this [create trust] by stressing the idea that anyone can be assimilated, that everyone should have a chance, that mass culture can give all people something in common, and that citizenship imposes similar obligations on everyone" (Fallows 1989, 26). This is the American genius.

Global education embodies the best qualities of these democratic citizenship characteristics. This shared understanding is largely the reason that global education partnerships, properly construed and developed, can generally overcome sharp divisions between schools and universities. In Chapter 9 of this book, Toni Fuss Kirkwood offers case studies that demonstrate the psychological bonding power of global education and its positive effects on school-university interactions.

Universal Applications

Alger (1986, 254-273) makes the point that global education is fundamentally different from past approaches to international education. Earlier efforts to close the gap in our international knowledge, such as language and area studies under NDEA, tended to "be separate additions to existing programs, often even housed outside regular academic units." Consequently, these programs had little effect on the separate disciplines and the professional schools, which went about their business as before. Dependent on outside funding, these units frequently disappeared when the funding ran out.

Alger correctly argues that global education is fundamentally different from these previous international education efforts because the impact of global education is much more pervasive in terms both of its content applications and the breadth of the people it reaches.

117

[First] the implication [of global education] is that all professionals and bodies of knowledge must in some way be prepared to deal with their involvement in worldwide systems. Thus, global education is not just something to be added to the existing curricula. Rather, it requires the removal of the national border as a barrier in education at all levels, and in all subjects.

A second difference between global education and past approaches to international education is the fact that global education tends to be viewed as a necessity for everybody. Although not usually asserted as explicit practice, international education in the past was actually available only to a small elite, and teaching and research focused primarily on the activities of a few officials in national capitals. No longer can professional preparation for world affairs be limited to those in political science and economics who desire to occupy posts in the "foreign policy establishment." Doctors, dentists, nurses, lawyers, teachers, journalists, bankers, businesspersons, agronomists, and so forth are all involved in world affairs, both as professionals and as private persons. Plumbers, electricians, carpenters, and workers in factories, office stores, restaurants, and so forth are also similarly involved. All have a need to know in what ways they are involved, how they are affected and how they affect people in other countries (Alger 1986, 257).

The idea that global education is for everyone involves an important corollary about innovative learning: individuals and societies must be prepared to act in concert in new situations, especially those created by the human mind and hand. Innovative learning, according to Botkin and others (1979), "is an indispensable prerequisite to resolving any of the global issues." To bridge the human gap between the "world problematic"—the enormous tangle of problems in sectors such as energy, population, and food that confront us with great complexity—and our current knowledge and ability to take action, we need to engage in innovative learning. Innovative learning can be modeled in a school-university partnership and can serve as a guide for global classroom instruction.

Innovative learning includes two primary features: anticipation and participation. Anticipation, in contrast to adaptation, prepares for contingencies and proposes and evaluates future alternatives. It encourages participants to consider trends, to make plans, to evaluate future consequences, to look for possible negative side effects of decisions, and to look for the global linkages to local problems. Participation involves shared problem identification, problem solving, and decision making. The broadest possible spectrum of participation is desirable to hear the ideas of all and to mitigate against being blindsided by some surprise. Participation requires an extension of the circle of trust mentioned earlier. The participation mode of decision making means that power cannot be used arbitrarily to block innovative learning.

Reich (1989) postulates that for the United States to meet the challenges of the new global economy, creative participation by everyone will be required. An education system modeled around long lists of facts to be committed to memory, standardized testing, and tracking practices is counterproductive.

What is needed is an education designed to foster greater anticipation and participation by *all* students in the learning process. Only then will students acquire the characteristics of mind and heart needed to formulate problems and questions, and develop the skills of collaboration required to solve these problems in an interdependent and complex world. Global education offers a rationale for according high priority to this kind of innovative learning and provides a conceptual framework for developing the necessary educational means to achieve these now necessary, but not entirely new, ends of education.

Examples of innovative learning and decision making abound in nations attempting to compete in the global economy. Some of the best known examples come from Japan, whose dynamic performance is leading all nations into the 21st century. The worldwide success of products made in Japan may largely be due to the anticipation of cultural and geographical variation in market demands around the world. Toyota, for example, prides itself in developing cars that fit local tastes and environments. Moreover, Toyota employees are constantly and productively participating in the decisions about the manufacturing procedures and marketing strategies, thereby ensuring a high-quality product. The official motto of the Toyota Corporation (1988) is: "But What Did You Do For Me Tomorrow?" Of much greater surprise is Mikhail Gorbachev's *perestroika* and *glasnost*, which have involved measurably more anticipation and participation by the average Russian than during the totalitarianism of the Stalin era. The driving force behind the Soviet Union's about face is the realization that a much greater degree of participation by ordinary citizens is required if the country wishes to remain a major world power. Serious obstacles to innovation are being removed, such as revealing the legacy of Stalin's terror and opening up a society tightly closed to the rest of the world. Lech Walesa's successful effort in Poland to obtain official recognition of Solidarity is yet another example of anticipation and participation in the political-economic sphere.

School-university partnerships for global education offer the opportunity to foster global education for everyone; indeed, global education designed for the elite is a serious contradiction between philosophy and practice. Global education has great promise for creating greater access by all to knowledge about the world, a deficiency that Goodlad (1984) found to be among the most serious shortcomings of American education. School-university partnerships provide a hands-on opportunity for testing the validity and the staying power of innovative learning through anticipatory and participatory classroom experiences.

Mutual Rewards

Like most worthwhile efforts, the development of a successful and mature school-university partnership takes time. It also requires patience and perseverance, especially because the trust gap is frequently wide and the risk of failure is great. Many of the deeper rewards of a school-university partnership emerge only after an initial period of development.

An example of what is meant by a "deep reward" is the opportunity for personnel in both the schools and universities to have immediate and personal access to the multitude of resources of the other partner. This can occur only after two or three years of continuous and successful effort to build up the trust relationship. For example, a great benefit for the university is the opportunity to conduct cooperative research in the schools with a minimum of bureaucratic hurdles and to be able to capitalize on the technical research capacity that exists in many school systems. For the schools, deep rewards mean instant and personal access to the resources of the university, ranging from library materials and advice by professors to convenient space for meetings, seminars, and workshops. These resources cannot be provided as easily, conveniently, or systematically by third parties or by outside consultants who lack a proximal and sustained institutional base.

One example of functioning partnership has been the CHI project, which has served to link Chapman College with 11 schools in eight school districts. Key to the research aspects of the program has been the involvement of four faculty members at the college. On the service side, eight faculty members have participated in one way or another over the four-year life of the project. Represented in such activities have been departments of art, education, history, political science, and sociology. All potential teacher education graduates receive instruction in global education, and many secondary student teachers are placed in network schools with teachers who are developing curriculums with a global perspective. Occasional inservice programs that carry salary credit for teachers have been offered, and a variety of material resources has been provided to participating teachers.

The greatest reward for both parties comes from the knowledge that teachers and students in both the schools and the university are gaining benefits from a global education program. This kind of professional satisfaction outweighs any kind of material reward that may result, although these are important, too. One example of an activity that provides such satisfaction is the creation in 1989 of a model United Nations to be held annually on the campus of Florida International University. This is a joint effort among the College of Education's Global Awareness Program, the Department of Political Science, the university's Student Government Association, and the Dade County Public Schools (see Chapter 9, by Toni Fuss Kirkwood).

Convening over a two-day period in 1989, 187 high school students from the public and private high schools of Dade and Broward counties gathered on the campus to discuss global issues such as the Israeli-Palestinian question, acid rain, and the peace process in Central America. High school and university students participated side by side. It was quite successful and represented the best values of global education.

What was extraordinary about this particular model United Nations was the ethnic composition of the student participants. Eighty of these high school students (43 percent) were African-Americans and Haitian-Americans, mostly from Miami's inner city schools. This high percentage of participation by black minority students was made possible through the previous successful experiences of the Global Education Leadership Training Program in these same schools. The teachers trusted the university, and the students trusted their teachers. Consequently, students who typically had not participated in the educational activities of the dominant culture, except in athletics, and many of whom were on a university campus for the first time, participated fully in the discussions and debates about global issues. They were truly learning the skills of anticipation and participation. And the majority students were having a much richer experience as a consequence.

To have made this positive contribution in a city that has been featured worldwide for its racial disturbances was a great professional achievement. Although such an activity could have taken place in the absence of a mature school-university partnership, the levels of aspiration, commitment, and intensity shown by all participants are testimony to the partnership's contribution. Innovative activities like the model United Nations, made possible by a mature partnership, go far in breaking down the negative images that the schools and universities have of each other.

A second deep benefit of a school-university global education partnership is the opportunity to link preservice and inservice training programs. For example, beginning teachers in the secondary social studies program at Florida International University are required to take global courses in both their content field and their professional education strand. These students are then placed for their field experiences and student teaching in local schools in which (1) administrators support global education and (2) teachers and media specialists have received inservice training in global education. Thus, the beginning teachers receive global education support from globally trained mentor teachers. This arrangement reinforces the campus-based experiences as the most important factor in shaping the attitudes and instructional behavior of new teachers. The experienced mentor teacher also benefits from the opportunity to become a teacher of teachers, thereby providing a sharp focus for his or her continuing education in the content and the methodology of global education. Together, the mentor teachers, along with their beginning teachers, return to the university campus for at least one day during the year to receive advanced training in global education.

These mutual benefits are made possible because the idea of global education creates a shared vision and a common task, which together allay suspicion, build confidence, and open doors that are frequently closed in both the schools and the university. These are the building blocks of a new culture of cooperation between the two institutions.

Conceptual Framework

Becker (1982) points out that global education, just as any new field, suffers from a lack of an agreed-on definition, goal structure, and conceptual framework. However, there is no shortage of such statements in the literature (e.g., Anderson 1982, Goodlad 1987, Hanvey 1982, Lieberman and Rosenholtz 1987, Little 1982, Oakes 1985). The problem is twofold. First, the goal statements that do exist seldom provide a guide to practice, since most are ignored anyway. This first problem leads to the second. We need more experience in correlating goals with practice so that we can begin to clarify our efforts and be able to confidently define global education.

Despite the plethora of goal statements in global education, a successful school-university partnership must come to grips with this question of definition and conceptual framework. Participants and clients have a right to know the assumptions and premises of a program in global education. What counts in global education and what doesn't? This is an extraordinarily important and difficult task.

Members of local global education partnerships need to talk through their goal structure so that it fits the local circumstances. The grassroots character of global education, one of its primary strengths, must be taken into account; and the partnership must serve to promote the development of the individual schools that are members.

In arriving at a goal structure and conceptual framework for a school-university partnership, we must seek the widest possible input, including the thoughts of representatives from Third World nations. An advantage of the partnership concept is that such a diversity and range of ideas are readily available. Indeed, it may be that local areas in the United States are more likely to have a strong minority and Third World representation than at the national level, where such voices are seldom heard.

*   *   *

My final thought is to urge the development of locally based, school-university partnerships for global education. The times demand such collaboration. There are benefits for many groups in global education, especially for those groups that do not feel fully franchised in the current system. And these local efforts make a vital contribution to the national thinking about global education. As Kotkin and Kishimoto (1988) have pointed out, one of the nation's great unused reservoirs, as we face the less certain global tomorrow of the 21st century, is our cultural pluralism. School-university partnerships for global education can serve as a vital link in ensuring that we gain the most from these existing and growing national strengths.

References

Alger, C.F. (1986). "Implications of Microelectronically Transmitted Information for Global Education." In *Microcomputers and Education* (85th Yearbook for the National Society for the Study of Education, Part I), edited by A. Culbertson and L.L. Cunningham. Chicago: University of Chicago Press.

Anderson, L.F. (November 1979). "Some Propositions about the Nature of Global Education." Address given to the Social Studies Supervisors Association at the annual meeting of the National Council for the Social Studies, Portland, Oregon, mimeo outline.

Anderson, L.F. (1982). "Why Should American Education Be Globalized? It's a Nonsensical Question." *Theory Into Practice* 21, 3: 155-161.

Becker, J.M. (1982). "Goals for Global Education." *Theory Into Practice* 21, 3: 228-233.

Botkin, J.W., M. Elmandjra, and M. Malitza. (1979). *No Limits to Learning: Bridging the Human Gap*. New York: Pergamon Press.

Fallows, J.M. (1989). *More Like Us: Making America Great Again*. Boston: Houghton-Mifflin.

Goodlad, J.I. (1984). *A Place Called School: Prospects for the Future*. New York: McGraw Hill.

Goodlad, J.I. (1987). "Structure, Process, and an Agenda." In *The Ecology of School Renewal* (86th Yearbook of the National Society for the Study of Education), edited by J.I. Goodlad. Chicago: University of Chicago Press.

Goodlad, J.I. (1988). "Studying the Education of Educators: Values-Driven Inquiry." *Phi Delta Kappan* 70, 2: 104-111.

Hanvey, R.G. (1982). "An Attainable Global Perspective." *Theory Into Practice* 21, 3: 162-167.

Kotkin, J., and Y. Kishimoto. (1988). *The Third Century: America's Resurgence in the Asian Era*. New York: Crown Publishers.

Lieberman, A., and S. Rosenholtz. (1987). "The Road to School Improvement: Barriers and Bridges." In *The Ecology of School Renewal* (86th Yearbook of the National Society for the Study of Education), edited by J.I. Goodlad. Chicago: University of Chicago Press.

Little, J.W. (1982). "Norms of Collegiality and Experimentation: Workplace Conditions of School Success." *American Educational Research Journal* 19, 3: 325-340.

National Governors' Association (NGA). (1989). *America in Transition: The International Frontier*. (Report of the Task Force on International Education). Washington, D.C.: NGA.

Oakes, J. (1985). *Keeping Track: How Schools Structure Inequality*. New Haven: Yale University Press.

Peters, T. (1987). *Thriving on Chaos: Handbook for a Management Revolution*. New York. Alfred A. Knopf.

Reich, R.B. (January 1989). "Must Economic Vigor Mean Making Do with Less?" *NEA Today* (Special Edition: Issues 89): 13-19.

Sarason, S.B. (1982). *The Culture of the School and the Problem of Change*, 2nd ed. Boston: Allyn and Bacon, Inc.

Schein, E.H. (1988). *Organizational Culture and Leadership: A Dynamic View*. San Francisco: Jossey-Bass.

Toyota Corporation. (1988). *Annual Report*. Toyota-cho, Toyota City, Aichi Prefecture 471, Japan.

Tucker, J.L. (1982). "Developing a Global Dimension in Teacher Education." *Theory Into Practice* 1, 3: 212-217.

Tye, K.A., and B.B. Tye. (1985). "Incentives for College Faculty to Work with Schools." Paper presented at the Danforth Foundation International Education Roundtable, St. Louis, Mo.

Ward, B.A., and J.T. Pascarelli. (1987). "Networking for Educational Improvement." In *The Ecology of School Renewal* (86th Yearbook of the National Society for the Study of Education, Part I), edited by J.I. Goodlad. Chicago: University of Chicago Press.

8

Global Education and the Community

Charlotte C. Anderson

lobal education that taps into the local community is global education at its best. This local approach to global education offers an opportunity not only to enrich instruction and, thereby, enhance student learning, but to gain community support. It enhances student learning about "things global" by providing opportunities to explore global events and trends in their local manifestations. Hence, the impersonal and complex global issues are made more concrete and personal.

A community-based approach provides an accessible laboratory in which students explore ways universal processes and conditions affect human beings and are in turn affected by humans on this planet. Exploring the community to search for global links stimulates and supports a cross-curricular approach to global education. Along the way, students and their teachers learn more about their own local communities. When community members are actively recruited to contribute, parents and other community members can become allies in the pursuit of quality global education in elementary and secondary schools.

This chapter provides an overview of community-based global education and offers several examples of community-based global education projects, including the Columbus in the World project, in Columbus, Ohio, and the project sponsored by the Center for Human Interdependence (CHI) in Orange

County, California. The many instructional advantages of such projects include the fact that using the resources of the local community (1) facilitates curriculum decision making, (2) promotes and enriches cross-curricular application and achievement of goals, (3) identifies instructional resources that otherwise could go untapped, and (4) stimulates community support. One of the first such comprehensive community-based projects was the Columbus in the World program.

Columbus in the World

Research Background

The popular global education curriculums that bear some version of the title "Your Community in the World/The World in Your Community" can be traced to a research project conducted in the early 1970s by Chadwick Alger at the Mershon Center, Ohio State University. This political scientist and his graduate students conducted exhaustive (and, undoubtedly, rather exhausting) inventories of the ways various sectors in their local community of Columbus, Ohio, were linked to the world beyond their state and nation—in other words, into the global system. The sectors investigated included banking, medicine, religion, labor, real estate, research, education, agriculture, sports, media, and business. An early report of this project states:

> This is the first effort that has ever been made to obtain a detailed view of the international contacts of a metropolitan community across all sectors of life . . . . The goal is to stimulate more interest in international activity in Columbus by making people more aware of this activity. It is expected that this will make it possible for people to perceive more explicitly the ways in which they and their community are interdependent with the world. Hopefully, the citizens of Columbus will make more informed judgments about the ways in which their own community and job are interdependent with the world. They may also be in a better position to evaluate these activities in the light of their personal goals and values (Alger 1974).

In investigating the many ways that Columbus reaches out and participates in the world, the researchers found that in 1972, 29,000 tickets were bought in the city for flights from Port Columbus to foreign cities; $134 million of goods was shipped to foreign destinations (the primary products exported were machinery, scientific equipment, and chemicals); Columbus businesspeople made 1,190 trips to Africa, Asia, Canada, Europe, and Latin America; Ohio State University personnel visited 72 countries in all continents of the world; and area churches sent over $3 million overseas. In looking at the reverse of this process and identifying ways that the world comes to Columbus, they found that there were more than over 1,100 foreign students in Columbus colleges and universities; more than 7,000 foreign visitors were hosted by voluntary organizations, universities, and businesses in 1972; foreign artists appeared in more than 40 events in the performing arts in the city; and some 17,000 people who were born abroad resided in the Columbus area.

By going out into the community to acquire their data, these researchers began to sensitize community members to their global connections. By producing brief sector-specific reports on their findings and distributing them at community forums and other gatherings, the researchers significantly expanded on this awareness. The whole process was geared toward meeting their goal: "to stimulate more interest in international activity in Columbus by making people more aware of this activity."

In addition to the goal of providing people in a local community with a global perspective, the investigating team was also attempting to nudge social scientists—as well as other citizens—into recognizing that all citizens are engaged in international relations and in developing and conducting foreign policies; that the traditional bifurcation of domestic policy and foreign policy is in essence nonsense; and that responsible, participatory citizenship calls on all of us to address not only domestic issues confronting the policy but also foreign/international issues. The title of Alger's paper delivered at an international conference in Finland in 1975 succinctly expresses this broader goal. This paper was entitled "Liberating Publics to Perceive, Evaluate and Control the International Dimensions of Their Daily Lives."

In moving from awareness to critique and, perhaps, to action, residents of Columbus might, for example, look at the data on the many ways that activities in their city are affecting the world. In the process, they might begin to ask such questions as, "What are these chemicals being produced here in my hometown that are being sent abroad? Where are they going? How are they being used? What impact are they having on that local area, on the global environment?" Similarly, as citizens of Columbus become impressed with the many ways that actions initiated in distant lands affect their daily lives, they may be encouraged to pay closer attention to world affairs and accept their role as global citizens. Alger's work also sensitizes people to the alternative routes to international action that individuals and groups might pursue, noting the possibility of working through governmental and nongovernmental organizations at the local, state, national, and international levels. For example, in an attempt to stimulate tourism, citizens might work through their city government, through such nongovernmental organizations as Chambers of Commerce, through an international nongovernmental association—or go directly to foreign cities or nations.

Curricular Applications

Global Community Links. The first curricular application of the Alger project was in the fifth grade text of an elementary social studies series, *Windows On Our World* (King and Anderson 1976). One of its eight units is "The

United States in the Global Community," a case study of Columbus. The student book tells the story of the city's links to the world and directs students to consider their own links. The instructional guide assists teachers in directing students to search for global links in their classrooms, homes, schools, and communities.

They begin by looking at the labels on their clothes and other personal possessions. They rummage through toy boxes and enlist their families in identifying the imported items in kitchen cabinets and throughout their homes. As they bring their lists and artifacts, with identified countries, into the classroom, they map their links on large outline maps of the world. By drawing lines from "our community" to each of the identified countries of origin, the links become graphically clear. More imported items turn up as students expand their knowledge of sources of raw materials and the components of manufactured goods. The ancestral homes of families and relatives are documented, as are the global travels of teachers and family members. The media are monitored for the news of the world coming into students' homes and communities. The Yellow Pages of the local telephone directory reveal a full range of area global links. Forays into the community provide more evidence of global links as well as details regarding the nature of those links. Probes into community history reveal the ebb, flow, and impact of immigration from abroad. Not incidentally, geographic skills are developed, and interest in places "foreign" is aroused by this local-global approach to global education.

Secondary school teachers have readily adapted this basic model and expanded on it to suit their students and curriculums. Teachers encourage investigation into what is happening at either end of these global linkages—and along the way. Students seek answers for such questions as: How are exports from our community affecting living conditions elsewhere? How might a coup half-way around the world affect us?

Monitoring the media for international news provides an opportunity to consider how the public media in most communities both limit access to information and skew perspectives regarding other lands and peoples. Many classes have found that mapping media links over a period of time produces a map with several gaping, blank areas. The following questions arise: Does this mean that nothing is going on in these places of the world? How can we find out what is going on? Furthermore, those places that end up with the most links to the local community are most often places in turmoil. Strife is newsworthy. How does this news affect U.S. citizens' perceptions of those peoples and places?

To fill in the gaps and provide other perspectives, community people with links to these other lands are invited to come to school to share their viewpoints. Both the inventories and the analyses of the limitations and impacts of the local-global links will be enriched to the degree that community resource people support the students' investigations.

Curricular Decision Making. This discussion suggests the power of the community approach to global education to facilitate curricular decision making. It provides an opportunity to build on what Carlos Cortes (1980, 56-61) has termed "the societal curriculum," referring to what students learn from the society in which they live. It deliberately brings that curriculum to the forefront of students' and teachers' consciousness. Community/global education not only suggests to the curriculum decision maker what students can or cannot learn effectively from their surroundings, but also guides students to discover distortions or inaccuracies. Through investigating global education links in the local community, curriculum planners have a base upon which to build. They may decide to (1) give priority to some courses over others; (2) focus on given areas/regions of the world; (3) or emphasize certain economic, political, social, and historical processes. In some cases the decision may be to build on what is there; that is, to submerge students in the history and current developments of an area of the world that may be particularly relevant to the students simply because their community is strongly linked to it. Alternatively, the decision may be to concentrate on an area or areas of the world for which the community "links" provide distorted or scant information. Either focus (or some other) will be more legitimate than decisions made in ignorance of the current status of such access and information.

State Guides

Many state departments of education have supported the development and distribution of extensive units on the state's international links and activities. In addition to providing instructional guidelines, these units can be invaluable resources for data on such things as foreign investment and trade, population characteristics, ethnic settlement patterns, environmental conditions, and travel. The utility and vitality of such state-specific material is indicated by the fact that several of these have gone into second and third editions. The *Indiana in the World* material, for example, first developed and distributed in 1979, was published in a third edition in 1989. (See Chapter 4 of this book, by James Becker, for a more detailed discussion of state guidelines and other curricular resources.) The following global education project shows how specific courses of global studies can be incorporated into the curriculum.

A Cross-Curricular, Community-Based Project: The CHI Program

The CHI project offered teachers in their participating schools the opportunity to draw from a variety of activities under its "Your Community and the World" project, which was directed by a political science professor from Chapman College. This program, which was directly influenced by the Columbus in the World project, is described in greater detail in Chapters 5, 6, and

7. The following synopses suggest some of the ways that teachers of varying subject areas and grade levels incorporated the community-global connections approach (*Your Community and the World* 1986-1988).

Grade-Level Approaches

High School

1. Curricular area: English
   Unit title: *A Bit(e) of Global Fare in Orange County*
   Purpose/process: To foster an awareness of cultural interdependence within a community. The project provided students with an opportunity to go into their community to meet and interview owners of ethnic restaurants.

2. Curricular area: Biology
   Unit title: *Population Issues in the Local and Global Community: A Program Stressing the Interdependence of Mankind*
   Purpose/process: This unit was concerned with the growing problem of global population growth and its attendant problems of environmental degradation.

3. Curricular area: U.S. history
   Unit title: *Global Awareness Through Family Histories*
   Purpose/process: To help "American" students realize that they, too, were descended from immigrants; to help defuse racial tensions, eliminate racial and cultural stereotypes, and help the immigrant understand the "American" just a little bit better.

4. Curricular area: World cultures
   Unit title: *It's Our Backyard—Multinational Corporations in Orange County*
   Purpose/process: To help students increase their awareness of the role of multinational corporations in the community and the world.

Intermediate School

1. Curricular area: Language arts and world geography
   Unit title: *Tuffree and the World*
   Purpose/process: To investigate global connections within the local community.

2. Curricular area: English as a second language
   Unit title: *Folk Tales Around the World*
   Purpose/process: After examining several books and other sources of folk tales, students put into practice language skills as they wrote their own folktale based on their own ethnic backgrounds, which included Czechoslovakian, Chinese, Vietnamese, Hispanic, and Japanese.

3. Curricular area: Practical arts
   Unit title: *Different Lands, Different Foods*
   Purpose/process: To utilize the study of ethnic foods to help students identify ways in which their family heritages linked them to the world.

4. Curricular area: Crafts
   Unit title: *Ethnic Dress, Customs, and Crafts*
   Purpose/process: To identify and study the ethnic clothes, customs, and crafts of the diverse cultures represented by the students' backgrounds.

5. Curricular area: Spanish
Unit title: *How Interdependent Are We?*
Purpose/process: To build language skills while increasing students' awareness of the interdependence of their community and the world.

6. Curricular area: General
Unit title: *Odd Man Out—The Ethnic Child in an Anglo School*
Purpose/process: To have students of diverse ethnic backgrounds examine their roots, study schooling in the countries of their families' origins, and gain insight into the school environment as perceived by students of diverse ethnic heritages.

7. Curricular area: Social science
Unit title: *Discovering the World in Our Backyard*
Purpose/process: To increase students' awareness of the different cultural groups that live around them, to decrease the prejudice that exists between Asian and Latin American students. To research the needs of informants' families to provide appropriate assistance and to make beneficial referrals to these families.

Elementary School

1. Grade: six
Curricular areas: Language arts and social studies
Unit title: *Overcoming Cultural Media Bias—Research and Application*
Purpose/process: To have students evaluate if there is a cultural bias in television commercials. To explore the impact that television programs and their commercials have on children's perceptions of the world and on themselves.

2. Grade: seven
Curricular areas: Language arts, reading, social studies
Unit title: *Cultural Heritage and Links to the Community and the World*
Purpose/process: To enhance students' sense of personal connection with history, the community, and the world.

3. Grade: five
Curricular areas: Language arts and social studies
Unit title: *World's Fare—Six Ethnic Markets in Orange County*
Purpose/process: To take field trips to ethnic markets to make students aware of a range of different ethnic food products, the place where these come from, and preferences within their community.

4. Grade: one
Curricular areas: Language arts and social studies
Unit title: *First Graders Look at Community Members and Their Origins*
Purpose/process: To have students understand that all Americans have an ethnic heritage and to provide opportunities for the students to understand the heritage and ethnic groups represented in their classroom, school, and community by interviewing and bringing into the classroom parents and people in the community who have come to make their home in Orange County.

Community Handbook

To make community resources for global learning as accessible to teachers as possible, CHI staff compiled a handbook identifying global resources in the area. The introduction of the handbook reports that it "identifies programs, projects, and institutions to which [teachers] can turn for ideas, instructional materials, resource people, and other assistance as they work to develop global education" (Arambulo 1987). Similar handbooks have been prepared by global education projects for other communities.

Reactions of Students and Teachers

The potential impact of these learning experiences is suggested by the reactions of students who participated. One student reported that despite his initial lack of enthusiasm, he came to value the learning experience because "Other than finding just what countries are in our county, [the project] also brings us closer to them by letting us understand their customs and beliefs." A student who studied locally based, multinational corporations remarked, "I never realized the amount of connections between Orange County and the rest of the world." A high school student learned to see his community with an expanded vision as he reported, "The most common countries found in our county are Mexico and Japan, but you would never expect the countries of India, Pakistan, Thailand, and Spain are represented by stores." One ten-year-old, who was clearly amazed by his class trip to an ethnic market, exclaimed, "Boy! I feel like I'm in Saigon or somewhere!"

Teacher reactions included the following:

I learned right along with the students how far reaching our clothing's manufacture and fiber content was. We were connected to places whose whole existence students never realized.

I now read more news articles looking for global issues. I listen to the news on television to hear reports of similarities of cultures, i.e., the recent Moscow visit.

I enjoyed the project. It was encouraging for me and my students. It gave me the motivation to go into my students' background and pull out information from them that made them think about their native birth country and about their new country.

Several teachers at my school have asked how they could help their students interact with each other on a more positive note.

Local-Global Links in the Curriculum

The local-global connections approach expands the possibilities for incorporating global education into all areas of the curriculum. The link between global education and multicultural education becomes apparent as one examines these learning experiences that tap into the communities within our multicultural society to learn about the world beyond our country's borders. Foreign language study is well recognized as making significant contributions to the development of a global perspective; and the connection between global education and social studies probably has been more firmly established than has the connection with the other curricular areas elaborated on here. (Again, see Chapter 4 by James Becker.)

Global projects such as Columbus in the World and the CHI program have provided the impetus for teacher—and student—creativity in enriching the curriculum, not only in foreign languages and social studies, but also in language arts, science, the fine arts, and other subject areas.

Language Arts and Journalism

The preceding curricular units suggest some of the ways teachers can use the local-global connections approach to teach language arts. Here are others.

Interviewing and Reporting. Journalism teachers should be able to devise several interesting adaptations of the assignment given by a university journalism professor to his undergraduate class on magazine writing. The students were assigned the task of researching and writing stories on the international links of the community in which their university is based. The resulting reports read as though they might be the human-interest stories behind an Alger-like study of the community in the world.

One student interviewed local realtors to gather information on some of the problems facing families moving into the community from other countries. His investigation led to his discovery of an area organization called International Orientation Resources, which assists executives of client companies in their move into the area. Another student reported on the involvement of local synagogues in the sanctuary movement and wrote a moving profile of a Guatemalan family who received refuge. Another student turned his attention to local record stores, where the international music stock is increasing due to popular demand, and clerks are challenged by a plethora of languages. The title of "the latest release from the hottest new group based out of Bulgaria" was perplexing one clerk, who finally gave up and concluded, "Well, the English translation is something like 'The Mysteries of Bulgaria.'" Another student reporter ferreted out a veritable Romanian Folk Art Museum in the attic of a home in a residential district. Still another interviewed the Korean owner of a flower shop that supplied localities with fresh flowers from such diverse locations as Holland, Israel, Columbia, and Mexico.

Engaging the Local Newspaper in Global Education. The utility of using the local newspaper for the purposes of global education has already been discussed. This approach, however, can be greatly enriched through the development and use of a curricular guide directly related to the local newspaper. In 1975-76, the Newspaper in Education Program of *The Peoria Journal Star* created what may have been the first such guide stimulated by the Columbus in the World project.

During the summer of 1975, three area teachers began working with Sallie Whelan, director of the newspaper's Educational Services, to develop the guide. Reporting on the project in *Social Education*, Whelan wrote, "We started clipping the newspaper during the summer, with the hope that we might have something started before school began. We were amazed at how much we found merely in routine stories about everyday life. Our problem turned out to be when to stop clipping." As they clipped, the teachers generated "ideas and planned student activities that could be integrated into almost every subject area and used at different grade levels. These included reading, writing, spelling, history, geography, mathematics, and science lessons" (Whelan 1977, 20-21). The resulting product was a spiral-bound booklet with photocopies of newspaper articles accompanied by teaching suggestions. The clippings and lessons are organized into sections dealing with immigrants, industry, agriculture, culture, science, and government. The guide, however, was not intended to be an end in itself. Rather, it was intended to be catalytic—to sensitize teachers to the global content of the media and encourage them to engage students in an ongoing study of the newspaper.

English as a Second Language and Language Arts. Many schools across the United States face the continuing challenge of receiving, assimilating, and educating large percentages of refugee and immigrant children. When this challenge is turned into a stimulating instructional asset such as was accomplished in Boulder, Colorado, both the schools and communities benefit. In the early 1980s, Boulder High School had a significant number of recently arrived Southeast Asian students, principally Hmong, in its student body. As a central project of the English as a second language (ESL) class in which more than 30 Hmong students were registered and 6 peer tutors assisted, the students participated in a Foxfire-like experience in interviewing Hmong community members and producing a magazine they titled *Worldwinds*.

These words from the preface suggest the learning goals:

> Designed to improve students' written and oral communication skills, this multicultural studies project is also predicated on fostering *community relationships* [emphasis added] and enhancing the job-related skills of the participating young people. . . . The students are also able to learn and share information about their own cultural and ethnic heritage with each other, and with the general public (*Worldwinds* 1982).

The process is described by the teachers/advisors:

> To write the stories, the students had to undertake a lengthy and difficult process. They began by interviewing their families and friends in their native languages, and then they transcribed their interviews from tape to paper. When this step was completed, they had the task of translating the interview to English, while attempting to capture the flavor and personality of the original interviewee (*Worldwinds* 1982, 40).

The resulting publication is a compendium of Hmong culture and experience. Article topics are suggested in titles such as these: "Across the Ocean: Pen Ouk's Sad Journey," "Hmong Marriage Rites," "The Shaman," "Farming in Laos," "Tong Via Xiong's Five Ghastly Stories," "[Student] Poetry," "Games Other Peoples Play," and "History of the Hmong—Past and Present."

Worldwinds sports a bright, four-color cover showing Southeast Asian children standing among the unfurled flags of many nations, including the United States. Inside are black-and-white photographs and drawings to illustrate and enhance the stories. The quality of the product is superior—and underwritten by outside grants. Such resources are certainly helpful, but they are not essential in providing equally rich learning experiences adapted from the Boulder project.

One can imagine, for example, a class project in which students with diverse cultural heritages interview older residents of their same heritage and compile the resulting stories into a multiculturally focused publication. Another variation would be the pairing of an ESL student and a native English speaker to conduct team interviews with community residents representing each student's heritage. Still other variations would be to obtain the assistance of community groups or businesses in the production and distribution processes—for example, securing the local newspaper publisher or a computer dealer to contribute the printing; asking the Chamber of Commerce or city council to distribute the publication; and teaming the community interviewees and the student interviewers to make presentations for parent-teacher groups, local civic clubs, and classrooms. The presentations would provide opportunities to go beyond the written stories and include sharing of cultural artifacts.

Science, Health Science, and Agriculture

The impact of environmental events originating in sites throughout the world are increasingly felt in our local communities. The converse is also true. Local experts or highly informed citizens can often be identified to assist teachers and students in not only better understanding these phenomena but also in recognizing how local people are involved in global environmental issues.

Consider, for example, what a rich learning experience could be designed by area teachers using the insights and expertise of community members involved directly or indirectly in any of the following events.

• In the summer of 1988, a South Carolina textile worker contracted anthrax simply from handling contaminated cashmere wool traced to sources in Afghanistan and Iran ("U.S. Reports Anthrax" 1988, 26).

• The sustainable agriculture movement (Gunset 1989) is curbing the extensive use of commercial fertilizers and chemical pesticides that characterized the Green Revolution of the past 40 years and is rediscovering and adapting many of the ancient farming methods practiced throughout the world.

135

Among the more exciting "new" agricultural methods is a rediscovery of one practiced in Peru by pre-Colombian farmers (Stevens 1988). Here an ingenious network of soil platforms and shallow canals enabled farmers to reap bumper crops in the face of flood, drought, and the killing frost of their 12,000-foot-altitude fields. Development specialists are encouraged by the potential for using this method in "less hospitable areas of the Third World, where flood, cold, heat, and drought routinely pose special difficulties, and where modern agricultural technology has not moved beyond the more favorable plains and river basins" (Stevens 1988, 19).

• Throughout the western rangeland, the seed head fly, imported from Europe, helps control knapweed, a rangeland pest. The fly lays its eggs in the seed head of the plants; when the larvae hatch, they interfere with the development of the plant's seeds.

• A small, stingless wasp imported from India is the scourge of the Mexican bean beetle and the salvation of many Midwest soybean crops. The wasp inserts its eggs into the Mexican bean beetle larvae and the emerging wasp larvae feed on the beetle larvae until nothing is left but the larvae shell.

• Local waste disposal is becoming an alarming global issue as toxic waste from U.S. and European communities is being dumped by waste brokers in West African sites (Brooke 1988). Where does your garbage go?

Exposing students to local stakeholders with diverse and conflicting strongly held perspectives on the issues inherent in developments such as these will convey both the seriousness and complexity of these local/global issues.

Art Education

Arts programs in schools are significantly enriched when they take seriously their potential for increasing students' international and intercultural competence and draw from the full range of the worldwide cultural storehouse. Such programs focus on examples of art that are an integral part of people's everyday lives, as well as examples preserved in museums and presented in concert halls and theaters. In ethnically and culturally mixed classrooms, it is especially important that teachers draw on the full range of the cultures represented by their students. In more homogeneous classrooms, teachers need to expand their students' perspectives of diverse cultural realities and possibilities. Tapping into the community's artistic resources offers opportunities to provide students with concrete examples of the artistic tools and practices of different cultural groups (see *Increasing International and Intercultural Competence* in press).

Each of the arts lends itself to this global approach. There will be as many variations as there are creative teachers and students in our schools. For example, music has great potential for a global approach. The earlier description of the journalism student's visit to a local record store suggests one local source for a link into the global music repository. The phenomenon of what the press terms "global pop" is apparently beginning to sensitize our young people to music from diverse cultures. It would be a shame not to use this burgeoning interest to increase students' knowledge about different cultures and societies around the world. In the spring of 1989, a Chicago radio station launched a two-and-one-half-hour Saturday evening program focusing entirely on music from around the world. In a local newspaper interview, the host observed, "This music is something in which everybody is interested. It's growing all over the world. . . . The show should provide people with an educational experience and context for this music" (Kogan 1989). What is coming over your local radio waves and out of your students' stereos and headsets?

One invaluable resource for multicultural music teaching materials is the World Music Press, which produces and distributes books and sets of tapes and books featuring the music of the world. For example, *Teaching the Music of Six Different Cultures* (George 1987) explores the "authentic traditional and contemporary music of Africa, Black America, Native America, Hawaii, Jewish song styles, Mexico and Puerto Rico," providing concise overviews of the cultural contexts for each musical heritage. One of the Press' newest publications is *From Rice Paddies and Temple Yards: Traditional Music from Vietnam* (Nguyen and Campbell 1990). Teachers who use such printed and taped resources *and* identify community people to assist in expanding cultural contexts will provide both rich musical and rich cultural/global experiences for their students.

Business Education

Members of the business community may be among the most globally conscious of U.S. citizens. This global consciousness is a direct result of the fact that American businesses are facing both a growing competition in the global marketplace and an increasingly ethnically diverse labor force. This global consciousness is fueled by the many analyses of the economic impact of foreign investment and trade to be found in publications of the business press. It is manifest in the "global twists" of advertisements and commercials in the late 1980s, for example: "The key to global performance is understanding local markets" (J.P. Morgan advertisement, *New York Times*) and "The business world has changed. It has become truly worldly in scope and sensibility" (Barney's New York advertisement, *New York Times*). It is seen in company manuals and signs that are published in more than one language. It is seen, as well, in business' growing sensitivity to alien employment laws.

Even relatively small manufacturers and distributors are moving into the import/export business. They are attending seminars on getting started in the businesses that are being offered by public and private economic development agencies across the United States. For the first time in their history, many companies are sending representatives abroad to scout out markets and products. In the process, employees are seeking help in developing their language skills and in understanding different cultural norms.

Local business leaders who are involved in the global marketplace will be valuable resources for many courses; but they offer a special resource to teachers of business courses. Their personal histories of evolving participation in the emerging global marketplace should convey to students the imperative for developing requisite competencies and for accommodating to change. Internships in these business settings would further develop students' knowledge of local/global economic realities and, it is to be hoped, encourage students to seek the competencies to participate in the context of those realities.

Physical Education

In physical education classes, folk dances offer cultural insights as well as rigorous exercise. Finding the answers to such questions as, "Who makes your tennis shoes and baseball bats?" will contribute to global awareness. Physical education teachers enrich their courses when they introduce students to games and sports of diverse ethnic groups and explore the cultural roots of traditional sports. An exploration of the games, sports, toys, and sports equipment that are a part of the heritage of the people in local communities will reveal many creative ways to use resources that are readily available. Introducing students to games and sports from diverse cultures that are based upon cooperation counterbalances the emphasis on competition that dominates U.S. sports. Many analysts argue that the skills of group problem solving, goal setting, and attainment gained from cooperative sports are essential tools for participating effectively in the interdependent world of the 21st century. The CHI-sponsored International Sports Day for seventh graders is a good example of this, because it involved students from several schools coming together to play cooperative games from around the world. On this day, students from five different schools gathered in teams that were combined and recombined several times during the day. Some international games they played were:

- Tug-of-war, which originated in Korea
- Hold-the-rope, from Israel
- Gora-gora, a flag game from India

In addition, the students played Earthball with a five-foot-diameter ball painted like the planet Earth. The object of the game is for groups of students to maneuver the ball up and down the playing field without scoring.

Home Economics

Home economics teachers have many opportunities for using community resources to expand global awareness. These include the study of foods and home crafts of diverse ethnic groups, as well as the alternative roles assumed by members of household groups around the world. Focus on household resource management and conservation—which is accompanied by examples drawn from diverse local households, as well as those around the world—will surely contribute to expanding students' perceptions of new possibilities. Have they thought, for example, of the possibility of braiding used plastic breadbags into kitchen and door mats or of creating dolls out of cornhusks? Have they investigated the local community's garbage disposal or recycling programs? How do these compare to the ways "waste" has been and is handled around the world?

For that matter, have they considered what is considered waste in the typical community in the United States and how that compares with the view of other communities around the world?

Mathematics

Local-global studies can be incorporated into nearly every subject area. One area that has received only incidental mention in this chapter is mathematics; but here, too, creative teachers will find ingenious ways to develop global perspectives. Mathematics courses that use economic and social statistics on the nations of the world, for example, develop students' mathematical competencies as well as their understanding of the world in which they live. Andrew Smith, of the American Forum on Global Education, admonishes, "Global education is no longer a question of having a fiesta or two to celebrate another culture. There should be international references in everything we do" (quoted by Fiske 1989, 19).

* * *

Engaging the community in global education programs provides access to an ever growing pool of globally connected people and institutions. It is possible, no doubt, that the community, in general, will not be aware of global education programs. It is likewise possible that educational systems will not take full advantage of either the educational or public relations value of using community resources. The community members directly involved may develop a better understanding of what has been termed "the global imperative" of education; but few others will reach such an understanding—unless involvement is consciously pursued as an explicit educational policy supported by the administration. When such support is forthcoming, more teachers will use the community; and community members will be better informed about the instructional programs of their schools. Mutual access can be facilitated through the development of guides to area global resources, as well as listings of teacher interest areas.

School administrations can stimulate this critical interaction by holding open forums in which community members learn of the schools' interest in local-global links and teachers gain an initial introduction to the extant pool of resources. Forums that focus on the substance of critical local-global issues will enhance both the knowledge base of educators and community members and their recognition of the value of such study in the curriculum.

The community-based approach to global education can help ensure that the education of our children is conducted in the context of an informed and committed community. One program that is dedicated to this objective is the Education 2000 project, which is a school renewal project designed by Willard Kniep of The American Forum. It involves a network that will include six school-community sites across the United States. The project uses the model for school renewal outlined by Kniep (1987). Education 2000 starts with the premise that if we are to prepare students for effective and responsible involvement in the highly interdependent and culturally diverse world of the 21st century, schools must engage teachers, administrators, parents, and other community members in addressing fundamental questions about the nature and purpose of schooling. As these educational stakeholders address the question of what students should be learning in light of the local, national, and global realities of the 21st century, they also address issues relating to their own roles and responsibilities for achieving these educational goals. By participating in in-depth investigations of the realities of the world for which students must be prepared, the stakeholders greatly expand their own knowledge of local, national, and global conditions.

A number of recent national reports, perhaps best highlighted by *The United States Prepares for Its Future* (Study Commission on Global Education 1987), call for decisive action by the schools to prepare the children and youth of today for participatory democratic citizenship in the next century. Many of these reports conclude that students not only need to be grounded in their own history and culture, but also need a sense of global history, an awareness of common human aspirations in a diverse world, and the will and abilities to tackle the great problems and issues facing all the inhabitants of our planet. What better way to address this critical need than by taking advantage of the multiple resources of our local communities?

References

Alger, C.F. (1974). *Your City in the World/The World in Your City: Discovering the International Activities and Foreign Policies of People, Groups, and Organizations in Your Community*. Brief Report No. 1. Columbus: Mershon Center, The Ohio State University.

Alger, C.F. (1975). *Liberating Publics to Perceive, Evaluate and Control the International Dimension of Their Daily Lives*. Columbus: Mershon Center, The Ohio State University. (Paper presented at the sixth general conference of the International Peace Research Association, Commission ll: Social Mobilization and Self Reliance, Turku, Finland, August 15-18, 1975.)

Arambulo, M.E.R. (1987). *Global Education Resources for Teachers in the Orange County Area*. Orange County, Calif.: Center for Human Interdependence.

Brooke, J.A. (July 17, 1988). "Waste Dumpers Turning to West Africa." *New York Times*, 1:7.

Cortes, C.E. (1980). "Multicultural Law and Humanities Education: Preparing Young People for a Future of Constructive Pluralism." In *Daring to Dream: Law and the Humanities for Elementary Schools*, edited by L.C. Falkenstein and C.C. Anderson. Chicago: American Bar Association.

Fiske, E.B. (April 4, 1989). "The Global Imperative." *New York Times, Education Life*, 18-19.

George, L.A. (1987). *Teaching the Music of Six Different Cultures*. Danbury, Conn.: World Music Press.

Gunset, G. (April 2, 1989). New/Old Way to Farm Rooted in Environment, Economy. *Chicago Tribune*, section 7: 1,7.

Increasing International and Intercultural Competence Through the Fine Arts. (in press). Springfield: Illinois State Board of Education and Foreign Language Leadership Council (a project of the Learner Outcomes Committee of the Council).

Indiana in the World. 3rd ed. (1989). Bloomington: Midwest International Studies Project, Social Studies Development Center. King, D.C., and C.C. Anderson (1976). "The United States in the Global Community." In *Windows On Our World* (Elementary Social Studies Series). Boston: Houghton Mifflin.

King, D.C., and C.C. Anderson (1976). "The United States in the Global Community." In *Windows On Our World* (Elementary Social Studies Series). Boston: Houghton Mifflin.

Kniep, W. (1987). *Next Steps in Global Education: A Handbook for Curriculum Development*. New York: The American Forum.

Kogan, R. "Play the Rock from Hard Places." (February 22, 1989). *Chicago Tribune*, section 5: 6.

Nguyen, P., and P.S. Campbell (1990). *From Rice Paddies and Temple Yards: Traditional Music from Vietnam*. Danbury, Conn.: World Music Press.

Stevens, W.K. (November 22, 1988). "Scientists Revive a Lost Secret of Farming." *New York Times*, 19, 22.

Study Commission on Global Education. (1987). *The United States Prepares for Its Future: Global Perspectives in Education*. New York: The American Forum.

"U.S. Reports Anthrax Case in a Human." (September 12, 1988). *New York Times*.

Whelan, S. (January 1977). "'Peoria and the World' and '[Your Town] and the World.'" *Social Education* 41, 1: 20-26.

Worldwinds 1, 1. (May 1982). Boulder, Colo.: Center for the Studies in English as a Second Language, Boulder High School.

Your Community and the World. Summary and Final Reports. (1986-1988). Orange County, Calif.: Center for Human Interdependence.

9

Global Education as an Agent for School Change

Toni Fuss Kirkwood

This chapter reflects the perspective of a bicultural, bilingual classroom teacher who has been given the opportunity to plan, design, and implement a global education program in 164 of the 263 Dade County Public Schools in Florida. It is based on direct contact, discussions, and experiences with school-site administrators, teachers, staff, and students over a six-year period. I have also drawn from in-depth interviews of students, teachers, and administrators in three schools in which global education programs were implemented across the disciplines.[*]

My purpose in discussing these programs is to examine why global education has become an effective agent for school change and to describe a series of interdisciplinary approaches to global education programs. Case studies of two schools illustrate specific strategies and methods used to implement global education programs. The third school is a new magnet school for modern languages and is discussed separately.

---

[*]I would like to thank the following individuals for giving of their time to provide information about the schools and communities discussed in this chapter: Von Beebe, Principal, Frances S. Tucker Elementary School, Coconut Grove; Dorothy Fields, Founder, Black Archives, Caleb Center, Miami; Fran Garner, Media Specialist, Frances S. Tucker Elementary School; Lois Lindahl, Principal, North Dade Center of Modern Languages, North Miami; and Barbara Silver, Principal, Miami Sunset Senior High School, Miami, Florida.

Miami is the oldest and largest of the 27 Dade County municipalities that stretch contiguously between the Atlantic Ocean on the east and the Everglades on the west, and are bordered by Broward County in the north and Monroe County in the south. Many people refer to Dade County as simply Miami.

There is an endless fascination with Miami. Some have called it the Casablanca of the United States: city of intrigue, refugees, and high rollers. The novelist Russell Banks has likened South Florida to a cultural "fault line," where immigrants from North and South rub together as two continents— sometimes creating cultural volcanos and earthquakes (Banks 1985). Without question, Miami occupies a prominent place on the world map—glistening in the eternal sun and under swaying palm trees where the traveller encounters a rich blend of cultures and languages and one of America's prominent dichotomies of simultaneous affluence and poverty.

Miami's school system is also a source of fascination. The Dade County Public School District, which includes the city of Miami, is the fourth largest U.S. school system, after New York, Chicago, and Los Angeles. It serves more than 280,000 students, who are taught by more than 15,000 teachers. The annual operating budget to administer the 263 elementary and secondary schools exceeds $1.4 billion. The system serves students from 136 different countries. Located in a multiethnic, multicultural, and multilinguistic cosmopolitan community, Miami has become a microcosm of the world. And so have its schools.

Miami Beach Senior High School, for example, boasts the most diverse student population with 67 different nationalities; Miami Edison Senior High has 40 different student ethnicities. Coral Way Elementary School, on the other hand, is predominantly Hispanic—and all classes are taught in English in the morning and in Spanish in the afternoon. Northwestern Senior High School is 98 percent African-American; and Miami Senior High School is 97 percent Hispanic.

To be a teacher or administrator in Miami's schools requires total commitment to meet the needs of a constantly changing student population, with its diverse ethnicities, cultures, and languages. Indeed, dozens of different languages and dialects echo in the school halls across the county. Furthermore, many children who are Nicaraguan refugees served in armies rather than being taught reading and writing. So how do we teach the children of Dade County? To at least partially answer this question, I will present brief case studies from two schools in Dade County.

Case Studies

Frances S. Tucker Elementary School

Frances S. Tucker Elementary School is located in Coconut Grove, Florida, one of Dade County's municipalities. According to Miami's Black Archives, the school was named after Frances S. Tucker, a dynamic educator who was the first African-American principal in the state of Florida. Tucker studied under Booker T. Washington at Tuskegee Institute. Because of the influence of Washington's philosophy of education, Tucker instituted vocational studies at what was then a senior high school. In the 1960s, with desegregation laws and population changes, Tucker School became an integrated elementary school.

Today, the Coconut Grove community still bears witness to America's former segregation laws. Main Street divides black and white residents. Public housing complexes occupied by African-Americans in borderline poverty can be found next to an affluent white neighborhood with the majority of its homes nestled along Biscayne Bay, surrounded by a luscious tropical environment and hidden from the public eye. It is important to note that some of the affluent residents today are black professionals, and there is also an emerging black middle class.

The majority of the 550 students at Tucker Elementary School live in the public housing complexes and frame houses located in close proximity to the school. Several wooden steeples of old Baptist churches dot the neighborhood. Another dynamic principal, Von Beebe, with a faculty and staff of 40, directs the school's daily affairs.

The two-story school surrounds an angular courtyard ideally placed for many outdoor school activities. Each classroom is accessible from the outside. Tropical plants and new wrought-iron benches decorate the immaculate school grounds.

Since 1985, Tucker Elementary School has participated in the Global Education Leadership Training Program, a partnership between the Global Awareness Program, College of Education, Florida International University, and the Bureau of Education, Dade County Public Schools. In the second year of the program, the faculty council, as part of the school district's merit school program, voted to infuse global awareness into the existing curriculum.

Global Awareness Program. The school's faculty decided to study one country in each of five continents and two countries in Europe. The kindergarten class studied Kenya; first-graders, Brazil; second-graders, Australia; third-graders, Ireland; fourth-graders, China; fifth-graders, the United States; and sixth-graders, France. Each grade level was obligated to collect information and prepare a booklet, which included the basic geographic, cultural, economic, social, religious, and political features of the assigned country. A "Survival Kit" was prepared that included several helpful vocabulary words of that country's official language. A Tucker Passport was developed and issued to each student. As the student passed the test about the information learned about that country and knew the contents of the "Survival Kit," the student's passport was stamped, and the learner became eligible to participate in the schoolwide activities held each month for the different countries.

While the busy teachers taught their students, prepared the booklet, and tested their students' knowledge, they designed and planned special activities held each month for a different country studied. Since the cultural aspects of the countries were stressed, ethnic foods and traditional clothing of the people under study had to be prepared. The country's music, folktales, and special customs were studied, and presentations and performances were planned.

The media specialist, the parents, and the community became active participants in the global awareness program. Indeed, the media specialist became the researcher, producer of resources, and general supporter for the teachers. Regular daily readings in the media center with different classes involved folktales, poetry, and geographic identification of the cultures studied. A bibliography of available resources for each country was made available to teachers. Displays and global perspective maps decorated the library. Along with the classrooms, the media center became the major center of global activities. Special games were developed by the media specialist in which children had to identify the country of origin of various souvenirs displayed in the library. Other games included naming the 50 states of the United States and calculating international time in Dublin, Paris, Moscow, Nairobi, Beijing, Sidney, and Brasilia in relation to Miami.

A highly successful event occurred during the study of Ireland: The huge unabridged dictionary became the "Blarney Stone." After viewing a film on Ireland that taught how to conduct the ceremony of kissing, the children gave it a try right in the library by kissing the "Dictionary Blarney Stone."

Parents also became active participants in the globalization of the school. They sewed costumes, prepared ethnic dishes, and collected artifacts and souvenirs for the media center contests. Community organizations provided guest speakers, lent valuable artifacts, and sent representatives to the monthly schoolwide events.

The school cafeteria prepared ethnic meals for each country under study. Examples included Irish stew, French croissants, and Chinese vegetables and rice. The food was eaten according to that country's eating style. Learning to eat with chopsticks was a major event for the eager youngsters. A pedagogically important activity in the cafeteria included the distribution of food to the children according to the economic wealth of individual nations. The discussion following this event included sophisticated cognitive concepts. Examples include the inequitable distribution of resources in third-world nations and the absence of a balanced diet in developing nations.

The final celebrations surpassed all expectations for attendance and enthusiasm. Special invitations went out to the district office administrators, community organizations, and parents for this culminating activity of the year. The students, dressed in native costumes, "flew" on "Tucker Airways" to the various countries around the world--the classrooms were turned into Australia, Brazil, China, Ireland, France, Kenya, and the United States. They listened to the music of each country and ate its food. Singing, dancing, and games representative of the countries studied throughout the school year concluded the final celebrations and one of the busiest years ever at Frances S. Tucker Elementary School.

Student Learning Outcomes. All 550 students at Tucker School were tested. The pretests and post-tests were composed of test items based on the mastery of basic skills in world geography and cultural awareness, as outlined in the Dade County Balanced Curriculum Objectives K-6. The test items increased in number and difficulty with each grade level. The posttest indicated a 99 percent increase in student achievement at all grade levels.

In addition, each student's "Tucker Passport" recorded that the student passed the basic knowledge test about each of the seven countries. A final documentation was the "Around the World" scrapbook, which contained photographs and related memorabilia depicting the global education program activities throughout the 1986-87 school year.

Leadership and Collaboration. This case study demonstrates that "globalizing" the curriculum can make an impact on an entire school. The governing council, composed of teachers and the media specialist, chose to implement a global education program on a schoolwide basis. Leadership came from the teachers, who spent many extra hours on the design, planning, and implementation of the program. The cafeteria and custodial staff also assumed an important role in supporting the teachers' plans. Parents and community organizations played an equally important part.

Media specialists are critical to the globalization of a school. They are the identifiers and purchasers of new resources. At Tucker Elementary School, media specialist Fran Garner was part of the faculty decision-making process. Her involvement also included reading-aloud sessions with students, with a focus on stories from the countries studied. Garner sponsored contests, met specific requests from classroom teachers, photographed schoolwide activities, and produced the school's official record book of all activities and events. She helped ensure that basic skills as well as imaginative writing and silent readings were an integral part of the program.

The administration assisted the teachers in all ways possible. Principal Beebe stated:

> The global education program generated intense enthusiasm for learning about our world community. This was true not only for our students but also

for teachers and other staff members. In addition, professional teamwork emerged.

At Tucker, the global education program demanded collaboration between administration and staff. Its energy and spirit were contagious, involving parents and the community; it unified faculty, staff, and students.

Miami Sunset Senior High School

Once part of the vegetable and strawberry fields of rural Dade County and close to Everglades National Park, the surroundings of Sunset Senior High School have changed to suburban neighborhoods of comfortable, two-story houses arrayed in neat subdivisions. Only the occasional horse farm or verdant nursery reminds one of the pastoral setting that was, not too long ago, dotted with fruit and vegetable stands for the urban resident taking a Sunday drive into the "country."

Proudly displaying the blue letters of the "Sunset Knights" is the contemporary building of Florida's largest high school. Serving 3,234 students, the school has a total of 172 classroom teachers, 10 guidance counselors, and a support staff of 26 full-time and 16 part-time employees. Principal Barbara Silver and five assistant principals administered and accounted for over $9 million of expenditures during the 1987-88 academic year.

In that year, the student population was composed of 44.4 percent white, non-Hispanic; 4.7 percent African-American, non-Hispanic; 47.4 percent Hispanic; and 3.5 percent Asian/American Indian students. A total of 913 students came from 63 countries around the world, including Antigua, China, Ethiopia, Finland, Ireland, Libya, Vietnam, and Yugoslavia. The majority of foreign students came from Colombia (171), Nicaragua (160), Jamaica (91), Cuba (75), and Venezuela (63).

In the 1987-88 school year, the Sunset faculty made three decisions:

1. To become a school-based management/shared decision- making (SBM/SDM) school;
2. To participate in the districtwide Quality Instruction Incentives Program (QUIIP).
3. To implement a global education program across the disciplines.

These decisions demanded major commitment by administration, faculty, and staff. The decisions, however, were reciprocal in nature and formed the basis for mutual reinforcement. The SBM/SDM decision provided a basis for autonomy and creativity with certain budgetary freedoms; the decision to participate in QUIIP provided opportunity to promote academic excellence; and the decision to implement a global education program provided the needed content to achieve the desired academic excellence.

Global Studies in the Curriculum. The QUIIP Plan was entitled "Citizens of the World: Wondering, Observing, Reading, Learning, Discovering Self, Community, Nation, and World." The objective of the plan, Project World, was to make the "Sunset Knights" more aware of the world around them. An extensive plan of curricular guidelines and global activities was designed by the 18-member QUIIP Committee, which consisted of one or two representatives from each department. The guidelines and activities were then shared at individual department meetings.

Sunset's faculty members were committed to making the global education program a success. Each department incorporated a series of global activities that resulted in many experiences for students and teachers. These activities were implemented in individual classroom settings across the disciplines and in major schoolwide activities:

• Business classes worked collaboratively with other departments in the typing of information regarding international trade and finance. They prepared historical documents and tables and graphs on populations and hunger in the world. The locations of America's multinational corporations around the world were discussed and plotted on maps.

• The fine arts department compared and contrasted international composers, artists, and dancers with their American counterparts and drew conclusions about the opportunities available to them in their individual countries. The keyboard classes held recitals on European masters and played the background music for the humanities classes' slide presentation on well-known artists.

• The foreign language department fully integrated the cultural, economic, political, and social backgrounds of countries whose languages were taught. The languages included French, German, Italian, and Spanish. The department regularly published a newspaper, *Le Soleil Couchant*, in French and English—informing students of international events and global cultural events.

• The health/home economics department culminated its study of marriage with mock performances of three weddings, each representing a different culture and involving parents and other members of the community. Child-care classes went to Miami's Metro Zoo and Sea Aquarium and studied the native habitats of the various animals. The world map was much used in this activity. The study of AIDS and its international scope was an ongoing, major theme. Finally, an international career fair of health-related fields was held at the end of the year.

• Thirty-eight language arts classes held recitations on cultural backgrounds and contributions of countries in Africa, Asia, Europe, and Latin America. Debate classes argued over controversial issues such as the homeless, censorship, the treatment of elderly people around the world, and the effects of world events on the local community. In preparation for reading *Julius Caesar*, students traced the Roman Empire on the contemporary world map.

• The math classes focused on hunger around the world and the distribution of natural resources and wealth worldwide. Students plotted the earth's finite resources in graphs and tables. Geometry teachers compared and contrasted shapes in different architectural structures throughout the world. The American dollar was converted into rubles, liras, yen, and marks. Celsius temperatures from around the world were converted into Fahrenheit, and the advantages and disadvantages of different measurement systems were analyzed.

• Infusing global education into the physical education department had special meaning: It was the year of the Summer Olympics in Seoul, South Korea. Classes observed and monitored the performances of the best athletes around the world and compared their own performances against them. World maps were used to locate the countries of competing athletes. Research reports included the contributions and backgrounds of the finest athletes. An Olympiad at the end of the year concluded physical education activities.

• Science classes studied new scientific inventions and applications or uses of scientific concepts. The department chair regularly placed current news articles into the teachers' mailboxes to assure currency of information and to raise "What if . . ." questions about the future. The science department sponsored Sunset's participation in a national weather experiment to determine surface and high-altitude wind patterns by means of a balloon launch.

• Social studies activities included a series of guest speakers on such topics as the international consequences of the October 1987 stock market crash and U.S. foreign policy in Nicaragua and its ramifications for the world at large. Teachers linked historical events to current events and to students' life experiences. Effective citizenship for the 21st century was the pervading theme in all social studies classes. Students compared attitudes around the world about euthanasia.

• Special education classes identified and constructed their own ethnicity graph of foreign students at Sunset. Then they studied the cultural similarities and differences of each country represented and made generalizations. Students celebrated Black History Month by studying selected former African kingdoms and their contributions to the world.

Schoolwide activities included the broadcast of major presentations into individual classrooms during the 35-minute Teacher as Advisor Program during homeroom period. Major televised productions were presented as a result of an interdisciplinary program known as the "Knight Traveler." These productions included:

Meet the International Student Body of Miami Sunset
Citizen of the World

Russia: Old and New
French Canada
A Guided Tour through National Parks around the World
Shakespeare's England
The Cultures of Austria, Germany, and Spain
Japan: The World's Leading Economic Power
Shopping around the World with Different Currencies

Thursdays were used for Sustained Silent Reading. The demand by students for an individual copy of the daily newspaper increased over 300 percent between January and May of that year. On Fridays there were national and international broadcasts presented by the "Knight Reporter." These broadcasts discussed major news events around the world and pointed out the interrelationships of events on a global scale. The hidden or "surprise" effects of an event and its consequences were elaborated. The use of wall maps in every classroom and students' own desktop world maps formed the basis of all global activities throughout the year.

Student Achievement. On the 50-item post-test, students showed a 89 percent increase in knowledge about the world. The test items were a compilation of teacher, staff, and parent suggestions about what Sunset's students should know. Sunset Senior High School was awarded the district's prestigious Meritorious School Award for the 1987-88 academic year.

Leadership and Collaboration. Principal Silver and the assistant principals gave the faculty its full support. Indeed, it was the idea of this far-sighted principal to suggest to the QUIIP Committee that the concept of global education was compatible with the philosophy and goals of the school. The administration also met frequent faculty requests for "reasonable" budget assistance in the purchase of materials and resources to implement the global education program. One example was the purchase and mounting of 7- by 10-foot world maps in the upper and lower lobby areas. These maps were labeled to show the 63 countries representing Sunset's international students. A third map was used as a backdrop in the television studio. Furthermore, the principal approved the purchase of a wall world map for each existing classroom and the duplication of desk maps for each of Sunset's almost 3,400 students. The instructional leadership of this creative principal proved to have far-reaching effects for students and teachers alike. Parents and members of the community supported this undertaking in full force. Indeed, parents and members of the community became an integral part of Miami Sunset's global education program.

Organizational Structures in Dade County Schools

In addition to individual school initiatives, Dade County has established two organizational patterns that have helped to foster global education. These are (1) the 25 feeder-pattern systems and (2) the globalization of a modern language magnet school.

The feeder concept comprises a "family" of schools, generally including six to eight elementary schools, two to three middle schools, and one senior high school. The purpose of this configuration is to provide students with an integrated scope and sequence for their learning as well as with the opportunity to attend school within a reasonable distance from their residence. With Miami's new emphasis on the SBM/SDM model, lead principals and assistant principals are chosen to promote an integrated approach to learning while using leadership staff in making decisions about the direction of their feeder schools.

The implementation of a global perspective into the curriculum of a family of feeder schools is increasing rapidly. The lead principal and assistant principal and their faculties of two feeder systems (North Miami Beach and Miami Southridge Senior High Schools) have decided to implement a global education program within a three-year period. The global specialists and master global classroom teachers of the Global Education Leadership Training Program are planning faculty presentations and workshops for administrators and teachers from all disciplines, including the guidance counselors and media specialists. The goal over this three-year period, which involves cooperation and commitment from administration and faculty, is the globalization of all schools composing the two feeder systems.

Principal Lois Lindahl of the North Dade Center for Modern Languages, which opened its doors in September 1988, arranged for global education training for the whole teaching faculty before her school opened. Before the beginning of the second year of this modern language school, the new faculty attended a four-day global awareness immersion workshop. This magnet school represents a true global school, in which all faculty members are systematically trained in global awareness. The school serves as a model districtwide.

Rewards for Global Education Teachers

The three schools discussed in the previous sections are participants in the Global Education Leadership Training Program of the Dade County Public Schools. The program is affiliated with the Global Awareness Program, College of Education, Florida International University. One of the major purposes of the Leadership Training Program has been to develop a cadre of experienced global teacher leaders. These global master teachers, who have received advanced training in global education, assist the global specialists who are permanently assigned by the Dade County Public Schools to the Global Education Leadership Training Program. This teacher-assisted training process enables the program to have widespread impact; in time, it is hoped, this process will help globalize all 263 elementary and secondary schools in the district. The institutionalization of global education in all schools of the Dade County School District is a major goal of the Global Education Leadership Training Program (*Global Awareness Brochure* 1984).

Since the inception of the program in 1984, more than 600 teachers have been trained in how to infuse a global perspective into the instructional process. That the program has attracted the very finest global teacher leaders attests to the growth and development of the global education program. This cadre of experienced global leaders will assist in the training of additional teachers.

Teachers are interested in becoming "global teachers" for a variety of reasons. Ida Urso, in Chapter 6, examines in depth why teachers in the Center for Human Interdependence (CHI) project in Orange County, California, chose to incorporate a global perspective into their curriculums. In Dade County, our experience matches that of the CHI (1986-1988) project *Your Community in the World*.

In the schools of Dade County, the goal of global education is to expand an individual's perception of the world. People with global awareness are sensitive to the multicultural and transnational nature of the human condition.

The intrinsic rewards for teachers with a global perspective are persuasive. The "global" teacher recognizes the importance of preparing students for the 21st century and is aware of the misunderstandings, stereotypes, prejudices, and conflicts that exist among members of the world communities. The global teacher is fully aware that the vast world has become a small global village. In addition, the global teacher meets the needs of the existing multiethnic, multicultural, and multilinguistic student population. Thus, teaching with a global perspective is interesting, rewarding, and meaningful.

Intrinsic rewards also come from the enthusiasm and new interest in learning exhibited by students. Exciting things happen in the classroom. For example, when the global teacher makes connections among the American, French, Cuban, and Nicaraguan Revolutions, he or she is linking the past to the present, about which students are knowledgeable. Some of them have experienced a revolution—or know someone who has.

Perhaps the most powerful reward is found in the positive contacts with other global teachers and the new or renewed contact with one's own administration and colleagues within and outside one's discipline. Where global education programs reach across the disciplines, a new collegial spirit and understanding develops that connects whole departments and results in stronger identification with the total school environment.

In Dade County, the global teacher is always involved when a school has the opportunity to participate in the SBM/SDM program. When many curricular decisions are left to the school, the global teacher becomes an integral part of the decision-making process. Because of his or her previous experience and leadership in the implementation of a global education program, the global education teacher usually assumes additional leadership roles. The teacher has input in how to spend some of the school's budget on needed resources.

Another opportunity for the global teachers is that of making application for small grants to Teacher Education Centers, the Florida Council on Economic Education, the Florida Geographic Alliance, or other sources. Because of a high degree of professional behavior, mastery of a global perspective in the instructional process, and the innovative ideas often found in global projects, the globally trained teacher usually is a prime recipient of grant monies. Grants have ranged from small amounts, such as a grant of $200 to take students on field trips in a multicultural setting, to thousands of dollars to write curriculums or equip a school with computers to work with students at risk.

Being chosen the Global Teacher of the Year is one of the greatest honors given in Dade County Public Schools. On the statewide level, the publishers of Social Issues Resources, Inc., Boca Raton, Florida, annually present the outstanding global classroom teacher in the State of Florida with a $500 award. In addition, the school library of the Global Teacher of the Year receives a $500 award for the purchase of resources.

Being one of the 28 global master teachers is another prestigious way to be honored for leadership, hard work, and professionalism. This cadre of global master teachers has the opportunity to teach teachers new in the Global Education Leadership Training Program as well as participate in decision-making processes regarding the global education programs in schools. These global teachers are also provided with substitute teachers so they can meet to discuss and develop global lessons for use in various content areas of the elementary and secondary curriculum.

It is further assumed that global master teachers, particularly those who are involved in the training of other teachers, have a good chance to be selected for the Fulbright Teacher Summer Study Abroad Program and other fellowships.

Conceptual Framework

The Dade County Global Education Leadership Training Program uses the Hanvey (1976) definition of global education as a basis for the training of teachers. (See Chapter 3, by Steve Lamy, for an extensive discussion of Hanvey's definition.) It fits well because teachers in Florida are bound by state-level curriculum frameworks and district curriculum objectives. Thus, in Dade County, as in many other places in the United States, global education is best approached through an "infusion" strategy rather than through the establishment of separate courses. The Hanvey model supports such a strategy.

In the process of globalizing the curriculum, the Dade County program has fostered the following kinds of classroom activities within the framework of the Hanvey model:

1. *Perspective Consciousness*. Teachers have been encouraged to have students compare and contrast such things as the roles of family members, treatment of the elderly, child rearing, eating habits, and courtship patterns across cultures. In examining social customs and values in different parts of the world, students gain insights into various perspectives and begin to see that their views are not the only ones in the world.

2. *State-of-the-Planet Awareness*. Teachers are taught to have students examine current events, to use maps to locate places in the world where the events occur, and to link the currency of the event to historical patterns and themes. Most important, teachers are taught to have students speculate about the future if events of such magnitude would reoccur. The "What if . . ." question becomes an all-important inquiry.

3. *Cross-Cultural Awareness*. With 136 nations and multiple ethnic groups represented by the student population of Dade County's Schools, teachers are taught to compare and contrast cultures and have students draw conclusions concerning the commonalities and differences of humankind. The commonalities among people around the world are emphasized. Teachers are encouraged to use student, parent, and local resources; to engage students in cross-cultural simulations; to invite guest speakers; and to develop pen-pal programs around the world.

4. *Knowledge of Global Dynamics*. This is perhaps the most critical dimension of the Hanvey framework. Teachers need to teach students to understand the *systemic* and interdependent nature of events and issues. Students should be taught to look for unintended consequences to actions; and they need to develop an understanding of how comparable cultural, ecological, economic, political, and technological systems work.

5. *Awareness of Human Choices*. In Dade County, global teachers emphasize the notion "Think globally and act locally." Class projects include adopting a nursing home; conducting an anti-litter, aluminum can, or paper-drive campaign; having a sister school in a Third World country; studying the plight of immigrant groups in the community; examining the various aspects of local problems such as homelessness, hunger, and poverty; and developing student projects toward the elimination of these problems on the local level.

* * *

In Dade County, global education programs have become a positive agent for school change for a variety of reasons.

First, the infusion of global awareness makes content relevant to students' own lives. The globally trained teacher draws relationships between historical and current events and speculates about the future. Current events make sense because their connections to historical events are demonstrated, and their effects—both direct and hidden—on other nations and people are explored. The automatic use of geography skills and concepts gives students a sense of place.

Second, the globally trained teachers are enthusiastic. The new approach legitimates innovative instructional strategies. The teacher has freedom to be creative and flexible. The teaching approach becomes more student centered. The teacher becomes a coach and facilitator, rather than being the center of attention, the "only one who knows." Teachers seem to feel rejuvenated and in charge, and students become more responsive.

Third, the globally taught students are enthusiastic. When teachers are enthusiastic about learning, students are, too. Moreover, when teachers promote student inquiry, reflective thinking, and participatory skills, learning becomes interesting. We see some students demanding explanations or staying after class for "clarification." Students' involvement in class discussions and their performance on tests seem to be enhanced. Student performance on post-tests has been significantly higher than on pretests.

Fourth, there is evidence of improved collaboration among administration, faculty, and staff. Teachers learn about colleagues they never knew existed; and bonding and unifying of faculty, staff, and administration evolves. A sense of common goals seems to cement relationships. Pride and sense of ownership have emerged, and an esprit de corps has become established.

Fifth, parents and community members have become involved in a variety of ways. In some cases, parents have provided leadership in carrying out specific tasks such as cooking ethnic foods or sewing costumes.

Sixth, global education promotes inter- and intra-ethnic understanding that leads to insight and appreciation of other cultures, their traditions, and their contributions. Global studies and activities help reduce tensions and conflicts in multiethnic, multicultural, and multilinguistic urban communities. Global education serves the international student population and its community.

The Dade County project is only a few years old. Already there are significant results (Kirkwood 1987). Similar positive outcomes are demonstrated in data collected by the Center for Human Interdependence on the opposite side of the continent. Because of these successes and the commitment of administrators, teachers, and district staff, an expansion of global education programs in Dade County schools will be a natural phenomenon. It is hoped that education leaders across the nation will join in this exciting and important grassroots movement that prepares students for competent citizenship in the 21st century.

References

Banks, R. (1985). *Continental Drift*. New York: Harper and Row.

Center for Human Interdependence. (1986-1988). *Your Community and the World. Summary and Final Reports*. Orange County, Calif.: Center for Human Interdependence.

Global Awareness Brochure. (1984). Miami: Global Awareness Program, College of Education, Florida International University.

Hanvey, R.G. (1976). *An Attainable Global Perspective*. Denver, Colo.: Center for Teaching International Relations.

Kirkwood, T.F. (1987). "The Assessment of School-Based Global Education Plans in Forty-Five Elementary Schools of Dade County Public Schools According to the Hanvey Model." Unpublished manuscript, College of Education, Florida International University, Miami.

Conclusion:
A Look
to the Future

Kenneth A. Tye

*I*n this book, we have presented what we believe is a powerful rationale for global education; at the same time, we have realistically described the difficulties involved in changing the curriculum of our schools so that it includes a needed global perspective. Such difficulties arise both from the controversial nature of global education and from the fact that there is a "deep structure" of schooling (common characteristics supported by society) so powerful that it almost defies change.

We also have looked at the practice of education by examining current offerings in the social studies, the role of principals and teacher leaders in the development of global studies, the value of collaboration between higher education and schools, and the importance of the community to the movement. We have examined global-infusion projects in individual schools. Throughout, we have emphasized the potential of global education as a vehicle for school improvement and renewal.

This publication grew out of a weekend meeting that began with the description of a global education research project conducted by the Center for Human Interdependence (CHI) at Chapman College, Orange County, California. The weekend meeting included an examination of data from that study. The weekend and the study are discussed briefly in the Introduction of this book, and most chapters refer to some of those data. Four themes emerged from the CHI data; I believe these themes tie together the ideas expressed in the previous chapters and suggest a possible agenda for future action (see also B. Tye and K. Tye in press). These themes are global education as a social movement, the search for definition, competing demands on teachers' time, and expansions of global education.

Global Education as a Social Movement

To speak of a social movement implies a program or set of actions by a significant number of people directed toward some social change (Gusfield 1970, 2). The United States began as a result of a revolution, which was part of a worldwide social movement, along with the French Revolution and others; this movement produced what has been viewed variously as independence from tyranny, the establishment of democracy, or the rise of bourgeois nationalism. America's history can be viewed as a series of social movements: Abolition, Secession, Temperance, Labor, Women's Rights, Populism, McCarthyism, Civil Rights, and Christian Fundamentalism, to name a few. Frequently, social movements are in conflict with each other, as is currently true with the Pro-Life and Pro-Choice movements.

Global education has many of the characteristics of a social movement. I have chosen to examine it in light of four of the commonly accepted features of such movements, as follows:

- Conditions that produce the movement
- Membership
- Sociopolitical context
- Structural properties

In this examination, I will use data from the CHI study.

Conditions That Produce the Movement

We began the CHI project by telling faculty members of the 11 network schools about the importance of global education. Although our presentation of a rationale for global education was nowhere as thorough as Lee Anderson's in Chapter 1, we described the changing world conditions with regard to cultural, ecological, economic, political, and technological systems; and we emphasized the need to prepare students for life in a changing world. Throughout the four-year project, we continued in one way or another to make participants aware of the need to infuse a global perspective into the curriculum.

In the final weeks of the project, we administered a questionnaire to teachers at 10 of the schools (the 11th school had been closed at the end of the third year because of declining enrollments.) One question asked teachers to agree or disagree on a 6-point Likert scale to the statement "Global education is important and all students should be exposed to it." Ninety percent agreed with the statement, and approximately one-half agreed strongly. Only 7 percent disagreed, and 3 percent responded, "I don't know." Clearly, teachers in this project understood the importance of global education.

We also asked teachers why they had become involved with the project. Though numbers varied from school to school, approximately one-half of the teachers in the ten schools indicated that they had been involved. Among those who perceived that they had been very active, 40 percent said it was because "I felt it was part of an important educational movement." Thirty-six percent responded, "I saw it as a professional opportunity," while the remainder divided their responses between "I wanted to meet and share with other teachers," "I sought validation or recognition of work in which I was already involved," and "I received monetary assistance to carry out educational projects" (this assistance consisted of small grant awards that were part of the program).

Eighty-two percent of the respondents agreed with the statement "I am more aware of global issues than I was four years ago." Sixty-eight percent credited this awareness, at least in part, to CHI's presence. Given the media focus during the recent past on issues of ecology, trade, terrorism, changing political systems, and so forth, it is no wonder that many teachers are sensitive to the conditions that produce the need for global education. Given the events of late 1989 in Eastern Europe and the Soviet Union, I believe that it would be easier now than ever before to interest educators in global education because the need is currently so obvious.

Membership

Nearly all teachers in our sample felt that global education was important and that all students should be exposed to it, but only 52 percent who responded to our end-of-project questionnaire indicated that they had been involved actively. (Everyone, of course, had been at faculty meetings where we presented information, and each teacher had received the project newsletter four times per year.) From interviews, we determined that nonparticipation occurred for a variety of reasons. Most people indicated simply that they were too busy with other things. Some saw it as the job of social studies teachers or, more specifically at the high school level, the world history, world cultures, or world geography teachers. Some said they didn't understand what global education was or didn't know how to implement it. Although few people admitted it in formal interviews, we know there was a small number of teachers philosophically opposed to global education.

The CHI project never focused solely on the social studies. We always argued that we did not want a new course added to an already overcrowded curriculum. We worked to "infuse" a global perspective into existing courses. This infusion model is the one that most of the authors of this book endorse. In fact, at the six secondary schools that worked with CHI, one-third of the teachers who said they actively participated taught English, language arts, or reading. Only 18 percent were social studies teachers, 10 percent taught science, and the remainder represented other subject areas.

The question arises concerning what kinds of people are attracted to a social movement. From our data, we would hypothesize that teachers who have lived overseas, those who began following world news early in life, and those whose parents discussed current events with them while they were growing up would be more apt to become involved with global education. Conventional wisdom often has it that older, more experienced teachers are less apt to participate in something new. Our data suggest quite the opposite. The teachers with whom we worked had a variety of backgrounds; but the biggest group, in terms of years of experience, was made up of teachers with 12 years or more. Also, it has been said that global education is a male-dominated movement because men are more apt to be concerned with external affairs while women are more inward looking. Sixty-four percent of the teachers involved with us were women, as were many of those who provided leadership to the project in their schools.

Finally, some individuals are attracted to social movements for psychological reasons, particularly if they have failed to achieve a satisfying status or identity with normal membership groups. The prestige and sense of belonging provided by a movement may be more important than the value of the movement (Sherif and Sherif 1967). There were instances of this type of involvement in the CHI project. In a few cases, people who identified with us early were seen by the majority of the faculties as being on the fringe—and thus, the majority had a tendency to consider global education as a fringe movement, also. In one school, the principal actually chastised us for giving a small grant to one teacher "because he was not accepted by the other teachers." In most cases, we were able to overcome any negative image simply by demonstrating that we worked with everyone.

Sociopolitical Context

Steve Lamy, in Chapter 3, described the sociopolitical dimensions of the CHI project. In addition, it should be pointed out that the network of schools was located in a region of the country wherein Christian fundamentalism and what Lamy labels as the ultraconservative "utopian right" position are both very strong. Fundamentalists see global education as a manifestation of secular humanism, and the utopian right sees it as a threat to the promotion of American ideals and values throughout the world. The fact that global education seeks to promote a realistic view of the world and the ongoing changes in the cultural, ecological, economic, political, and technological systems therein is lost on both groups.

Lamy, after reviewing the CHI data, suggested that we had little political trouble because (1) we did not push a particular worldview and (2) we most often dealt with less controversial issues, such as ecology and multicultural relations. We only infrequently dealt with more controversial ones such as arms control. In addition, we had no predetermined curriculum to introduce. Rather, we offered assistance to individuals and groups of teachers who had decided to globalize their curriculums. We promoted interdisciplinary collaboration in our newsletter and through our small grant program.

Two school districts chose to present the project to their boards and communities as something other than global education. One designated it as "international" studies, and the other called it "multicultural education." After surveying the faculties of network schools, we selected workshop topics, including global ecology, global economics, multicultural relations, conflict resolution, dealing with controversial issues in the classroom, folk art and literature, folk dance, and teaching global issues through literature. The small grants mentioned previously were given in response to proposals developed by teachers and judged by their peers. As mentioned in the Introduction, the networkwide programs designed by the CHI staff were (1) Orange County and the World, modeled after Columbus and the World (Alger 1974); (2) International Sports Day, at which middle school boys and girls played cooperative games from around the world; and (3) a telecommunications project in which classrooms in four schools had modem connections with classrooms in other parts of the world.

In one school district, a board member who also was a member of a Christian fundamentalist group expressed concerns about the CHI program from the beginning. The principal of the network school in that district met with the board member frequently. She and the assistant superintendent regularly forwarded written materials to the board member. We submitted to that district (and all others) a list of instructional materials checked out from our library by teachers. We had only one question about materials, and it turned out to be an inconsequential episode.

We did run into trouble with two of our many consultants. In one case, the consultant accurately described the changing world economic order in which American hegemony is declining. This was early in the project; and a group of teachers from one school who, for a variety of reasons, did not want the project to go forward, returned to their site and branded us as un-American. Subsequent events allowed that perception to be overcome, but the incident certainly impeded our progress at that school.

The second consultant who created controversy was contracted to discuss the special needs of immigrant students at one of the high schools. A small group of teachers there had done an outstanding job of surveying racial attitudes within the multiracial student body. The consultant addressed the faculty after the results of the survey were reported by the task group. Everything went quite well until she commented on the role of the Central Intelligence Agency in Central America. That one comment, made to a faculty with many politically conservative members, and combined with other factors, slowed the considerable early progress at the school.

In our end-of-project survey, we asked teachers to estimate the number of staff members at their school who were opposed philosophically to global education. Only 20 percent responded that there were none. Four percent said that the number was large, whereas 8 percent felt it was "about half" and 40 percent thought it was small. Perhaps the most significant finding was that 28 percent of the teachers chose not to respond. While Lamy is correct that educators tend to hold somewhat more reformist views than the general population, it is also true that teachers are drawn from that population and many hold comparable views. Some teachers in the CHI network were opposed to global education. They were not the dominant group, but they were influential on occasion.

Social movements, including global education, have a greater chance for development and growth in a society such as ours, in which we value freedom of expression and have systems of mass communication. However, a movement can be slowed and even destroyed by its advocates or supposed advocates if it becomes exclusionary or too limited in scope. Unfortunately, some global educators shy away from working with other groups interested in related issues such as third-world development, peace, hunger, or the environment. At CHI, we sought such collaboration and saw it as advantageous to reaching the goals of global education.

Structural Properties

Global education is a value-oriented movement in that it is part of a larger societal change that involves a new view of how the United States (or any nation) relates to the rest of the world. We are moving away from efforts to dominate others or export our values and toward a time of cooperation and shared values and goals. As part of this larger movement, global educators are dedicating themselves to helping others understand and adjust to these new norms in international relations.

In one sense, this move away from a competitive, individualistic view of the world toward a more interdependent, cooperative one is a major change for our society. However, viewed from the perspective of other values we hold— cooperation, democracy, fair play, and the golden rule—it is not. The idea that global education is somehow a leftwing movement is simply wrong. It draws on rich cultural themes deeply imbedded in the fabric of American society. As Boyte (1980) points out, Marxist theory calls for a radical rupture with the past, whereas American society has a tradition of social movement that builds on what has gone before. Global education is one current manifestation of such a social movement.

The Search for Meaning

Definition of Global Education

We have not spent a great deal of time in this book dealing with the issue of a "definition" for global education. In earlier days, at gatherings of people interested in the field, that was a favorite topic. This was understandable because in attendance at such gatherings was always a mixture of social studies educators, international studies scholars, social psychologists, educational policymakers, and teacher educators. Meetings of people with such varied perspectives always led to healthy and thought-provoking discussion. Such gatherings less often led to agreement on a definition of the field. It is my contention that the lack of a fixed definition is one of the major strengths of the field. As a social movement, global education is still developing; and it is interdisciplinary in nature. Because many people have a stake in its development, global education offers much promise as a vehicle for school renewal. Efforts to narrowly define the movement or constrain membership are misguided, at best.

Not everyone agrees with this position. Duggan and Thorpe (1986), for example, contend that definitions of global education are crucial to its integration into the K-12 curriculum. They cite Fullan (1982) who points out that definitions determine purpose and content, that they affect decisions made by educational policy makers, and that studies of educational change have shown that advocates and recipients of any innovation must have a shared meaning of that innovation.

At the beginning of the CHI project, we dealt with the issues of definition by referring to Hanvey's (1976) definition in *An Attainable Global Perspective*. We presented it orally and in writing at all early meetings with administrators and faculties. As Lamy observed in Chapter 3, this is a very general definition; it did not appear to be threatening to participants in those beginning stages. In reality, very few people actually internalized it to any great degree.

What we did, as Lamy noted, was to move rather quickly in the first year of the project to help people plan and carry out activities based upon whatever meaning global education had for them. This was a conscious strategy. Only after two years and much interaction with faculty members in network schools did we begin to frequently state our more precise definition which, we felt, was consistent with that of Hanvey. Here, again, is our definition:

> Global education involves learning about those problems and issues that cut across national boundaries, and about the interconnectedness of systems—ecological, cultural, economic, political, and technological. Global education involves perspective taking—seeing things through the eyes and minds of others—and it means the realization that while individuals and groups may view life differently, they also have common needs and wants.

A Point of View: Symbolic Interactionism

Our focus on *activity* and emergent meanings was consistent with our research plan. The plan was derived from a theoretical orientation known as *Symbolic Interaction (SI)* described by Kerckhoff (1970) as follows:

> The emphasis on definition and meaning is found in all works which emanate from the so-called symbolic interactionist tradition in sociology, the writing of George H. Mead forming the cornerstone of the tradition. . . . The famous statement of W.I. Thomas reflects both this conceptualization and the importance attributed to it by those who write in the tradition: If men define situations as real, they are real in their consequences (p. 83).

Symbolic interactionists study people interacting and developing common meanings or joint interpretations of events. They view people as being in the active process of creating structures, as well as being constrained by them. This is what makes social interaction useful in studying organizations and their development.

Social interactionism does not preclude the researcher from bringing to the site preconceived notions of human action. SI does not impose a priori theories, but SI does rest on certain assumptions. The term *symbolic interactions* was coined by Herbert Blumer, a student of Mead's. Blumer (1969) described the assumptions of SI theory as follows:

> 1. Human beings act toward things on the basis of the meanings those things have for them.
> 2. These meanings are derived from the social interactions one has with one's fellows.
> 3. These meanings are modified through an interpretative process based on continuing action in and interaction with the social world.

These assumptions have major implications for the construction of a research methodology. The methodology we used was described briefly in the Introduction. Essentially, we served as participant observers, we took extensive field notes, we analyzed and conceptualized from these notes, we returned to the schools and shared our analyses and conceptualizations, and we asked for the reactions of teachers and administrators in the schools.

It was through such a process that we hoped to (1) better understand the meaning that global education had for practitioners and, ultimately, (2) build grounded theory about global education as a strategy for school renewal.

Role of Meaning

In our end-of-project survey, we asked teachers to respond on a 6-point agree-disagree scale to the statement, "It is clear to me what global education is." They could also respond, "I don't know"; and 7 percent chose that response. Eighty-one percent agreed with the statement, with 28 percent agreeing strongly. Twelve percent disagreed. Most teachers felt that they had some idea of what global education was.

We also asked an open-ended question, "What does the term 'global education' mean to you?" Over one-third of the teachers did not respond to this item. A small number actually mentioned "learning about problems and issues that cut across national boundaries and about the interconnectedness of systems." Many spoke of interdependence or of understanding the cultures of others. One teacher said it was a Marxist threat, and two others suggested that it had to do with one-worldism. Most teachers gave simple, straightforward, meaningful responses. Here are some examples:

- Relating education to global issues, current events, worldwide concerns in an interdisciplinary approach.
- Understanding the social economic interdependence of all the countries with each other. We, the United States, are no longer the determiner of world policy but a part.
- No man is an island—we must work together to preserve the planet and the human race. Understanding each other—the world becomes smaller each day.
- I'm not entirely clear on the meaning. I believe it involves educating people to how other cultures in the world function and how that influences them.
- Awareness of how others live and their problems.

These responses are typical of those from teachers at all of the network schools. They all happen to come from the one school—which also, ironically, had the following response, previously mentioned:

It is a philosophical approach to studying global issues which promotes a one-world-type government at the expense of nationalism. It leans politically toward Marxism. There is much more emphasis on other countries than our own.

As previously mentioned, one school decided to refer to the project as being focused on "multicultural education" rather than global education. During the third year of the project, one teacher stated in an interview: "Until now I thought of it [global education] as multicultural studies. Now I'm beginning to see it as more holistic than that. It has to do with ecology and other issues too." This incident demonstrates the SI perspective concerning the modification of meaning over time. There are many examples of how meanings are derived or changed as a result of social interaction. For our purposes here, two will suffice. Many more examples are reported in a forthcoming book, *Global Education: A Study of School Change* (B. Tye and K. Tye in press).

At one middle school, we met initially with a small group of six teachers and the principal. As it turned out, this was the 7th grade core (language arts-social studies) team. They were very enthusiastic. In fact, one comment was, "We've just been here waiting for you [CHI] all these years." Indeed, after we had worked with them for a while, it was quite obvious that they had been teaching with a global perspective long before our arrival.

In the spring of the first year of the project, the principal, at a meeting of the 11 network school principals and district representatives, made the comment, "We've tried to bring in 'borderline' people so they can be moved along with the rest." My interest in and respect for Everett Rogers' (1962) paradigm of institutional change in which he identified "early adopters," an "early majority," "resisters," and so forth, caused me to wonder about the meaning of this comment.

Subsequently, I met with the principal to discuss the comment and to enlist him as a co-investigator in a ministudy at the school. We selected a sample of teachers to be interviewed and a set of questions to ask directed at finding out who felt ownership of the project. We found out the following:

• Teachers perceived that, to a degree, the principal channeled things having to do with the project through the 7th grade core group.

• These people were liked and respected, but there was some resentment among other members of the faculty.

• The 7th grade core group did get some satisfaction from their "ownership" of the project.

• A special project, initiated by members of the physical education department and involving games from around the world, had broken the pattern of dominance by the core group. This project was much respected by the faculty in general.

• Despite the "ownership" problem, the attitude of the general faculty toward CHI and global education was very positive. However, much of that was attributed to the respect for and popularity of both the principal and the core group.

We scheduled a feedback session with the staff, at which we shared and discussed these findings. In the months that followed, we saw many more teachers exploring instructional materials from our collection, attending workshops, and the like. The core group remained active, but ownership of global education became much more broad based.

In another project at an elementary school, we were less successful when it came to the matter of meaning. The first principal at the school was a very strong advocate of computers. He was in the process of developing an electronic bulletin board, and he saw the possibility of expanding it with our assistance. We did not participate in this project, but our discussions with him and two 6th grade teachers led to our providing funds for a telecommunications hookup between classrooms at this school and classrooms in Australia.

Initially, this activity included pen-pal letters. We had several meetings during a two-year period at which we attempted to encourage an expanded curriculum. For example, we suggested having students communicate with each other to build data banks that could be used to plan trips to each other's countries; and we pointed out that the recent celebration of our bicentennial and Australia's centennial provided an outstanding opportunity for a comparison of the constitutions and governmental structures of two western democracies. To us the computers were a means to an end. Although a new principal in the third year recognized this fact, the teachers involved saw the technology as an end in itself. Their position was reinforced by the fact that one of them received a special award from IBM, and they were written up in *Newsweek* for their work with computers.

We finally suggested that they submit another grant proposal. We indicated our interest, again, in various applications of technology to curriculum. The proposal that was submitted was solely focused on expanding the technology. They wanted a ham radio set-up. We did not fund their new proposal. Clearly, the meanings associated with the values of technology vary greatly in our schools. Such meanings, as well as those associated with groupings and interactions of teachers, can have a great deal to do with "bringing a global perspective to a school."

Competing Demands

Time for Participation

Duggan and Thorpe (1986) conducted case studies in two secondary schools that attempted to globalize the curriculum. They found that the lack of time to participate in inservice training programs, to disseminate new ideas to colleagues, and to attend professional conferences inhibited growth of interest on global education on the part of the teachers. Part of the problem was felt to be that global education was seen as an "add on," something extra to be attached to the curriculum, rather than as a different perspective to teaching. Moreover, inadequate resources for release time and materials were available. Teachers simply felt that they already had too many things to do in their classrooms. Time was the major obstacle to the implementation of global education.

This finding is consistent with ours. In our survey, we asked network teachers to identify what got in the way of their being involved with global education. From the possible 18 choices, approximately 80 percent of the teachers indicated "lack of time." Nearly 25 percent said "large classes," 18 percent responded "lack of money," 10 percent stipulated "lack of materials," and another 10 percent chose "lack of interest."

At one of the elementary schools where a great deal had been done to globalize the curriculum, we interviewed teachers specifically about competing demands on their time. Our question to them was, "What other competing demands were there at your school during the time CHI was there?" (three years). The following responses provide glimpses into the life of a busy school that took seriously the globalizing challenge:

> • The district expects a lot. Good district workshops to attend. Stressful this past spring, testing and conferencing with parents. Ordering (had $2,000

to spend). Never enough time to do it all. Preferred to focus on being with the kids in the classroom extra hours.

- Districts' interest in looking at new reading and math. Teachers were involved in aligning their curricula with these frameworks.
- Teacher commitments: Involved with new literature-based program, M.A. arrangements, meetings, personal things.
- Numerous. Experienced staff. Eleven mentors on staff of 16. Many active in association work. Several pursuing advanced degrees. A couple having personal crisis (divorce, etc.). Also, the specter of school closing. Anticipation and dread of how we do this.
- Biggest problem: no free time (4, 5, 6 grades). Fifteen-minute lunch.
- Staff development from District: textbook adoption in math, science. Also a child-abuse problem.

Accountability

The educational reform movement of the 1980s has been based on the industrial notion that teachers, administrators, and schools need to be more accountable. The press for accountability has taken many forms, including the required adherence of teachers to state curriculum frameworks and guidelines and the publication in local newspapers of school-by-school scores on statewide achievement tests. This is what one teacher meant when she mentioned "aligning curricula."

In California, as in many states, another manifestation of the accountability movement has been the lengthening of the school day and school year for instruction. Unfortunately, none of this added time has been allocated to staff development, teacher planning, or other professional activity.

On our end-of-project survey, we asked teachers about the effects of state curriculum frameworks and statewide testing on (1) their teaching and (2) global education at their school. Over half of the respondents felt that the curriculum frameworks were helpful to their teaching, but about a quarter said the frameworks were neutral in effect. About 15 percent responded that they didn't know, and less than 10 percent thought they were detrimental. The teachers were less positive about testing; fewer than one-third said it was helpful, more than one-third chose "neutral" as a response, just less than 20 percent stated that testing was detrimental, and the remainder said, "I don't know." These data, along with numerous interviews on the matter, suggested to us that network teachers were not overwhelmingly negative to testing. Rather, they saw it as a bother, only marginally worthwhile, and costly in terms of their most precious resource, time. On the other hand, a significant number of teachers did see value in the curriculum frameworks. That does not mean that they believed in alignment, because that time-consuming task is driven by a desire to get individual classroom curriculums in line with state-mandated curriculums which, in turn, are what state tests are keyed to. Thus, teachers are coerced into alignment to produce higher test scores for their classes and schools. This, then, is a powerful competing demand for their time.

In terms of global education, teachers were less clear about state curriculum frameworks and statewide testing. Only 23 percent saw the frameworks and 11 percent the testing as helpful to global education. Five percent saw the frameworks and 8 percent the testing as detrimental. The remainder were about evenly divided between (1) seeing both as "neutral" or (2) not knowing. From interviews, we determined that most teachers in the network schools did not perceive that either the frameworks or the tests reflected much global content. Our own analyses would suggest that this is certainly true of the tests; and, though there is some global content in the California Curriculum Frameworks, particularly in social studies, there is far from anything we would be willing to call a "global perspective."

Teacher Isolation

The explanation of why teachers, in the main, are not terribly concerned about state mandates resides in this interview comment: "Preferred to focus on being with the kids in the classroom extra hours." As Barbara Tye and I noted in our analyses of data from *A Study of Schooling* directed by John Goodlad (in which we participated), classroom teachers are little affected by influences from outside their own classrooms:

> Research on education change conducted in the Sixties and Seventies, clearly shows that 1) schools, if they are to improve or be improved, must somehow be connected to new knowledge from the outside and 2) conditions within the schools have to be such that staff members can share this new knowledge among themselves. However, these conditions do not exist in many perhaps most—schools today. Indeed, the reverse may more often be the case. The findings thus far from A Study of Schooling show that teachers are normally isolated from one another, that little in the environment or circumstances of teaching encourages deviation from conventional practices, and that teachers do not often come together in their schools to discuss curricular and instructional changes (K. Tye and B. Tye 1984, 320).

The pervasive norm among teachers of wanting to remain "behind the classroom door" (Goodlad, Klein et al. 1974) exists for many reasons. To begin with, the very structure of the enterprise encourages such behavior. Historically, education has been a "loosely-coupled" system (Weick 1976): Individuals, groups, and, indeed, schools have a great deal of autonomy. While this loose coupling is positive in that it partially mitigates against overbureaucratization and the recent proliferation of inappropriate top-down mandates, it does minimize interdependence and cooperation among people.

In addition, the tendency of teachers to work alone probably has something to do with the personal qualities of those who choose teaching as a career. After all, every teacher has first experienced the classroom as a student—whose teachers worked alone in the classroom. The role model of the individual teacher is attractive to many people.

Finally, the norm of isolation is reinforced by the way we build our schools. In most cases, each teacher occupies an approximately 30- by 30-foot classroom with a door, which is most often closed. Even in those schools in which there is "open" space, many teachers manage to close it up by moving cabinets, bookshelves, and other furniture into place. At the secondary level, we isolate departments by constructing separate "houses." Thus, there is a science house, an English house, and so forth. In large high schools, many teachers have the same students yet never meet, let alone plan together or even have a professional discussion.

The point is, the pervasive, overwhelming demand made of teachers is that they work in the classroom teaching their particular subject(s) in isolation from others. This view of how teachers' time should be spent is an important dimension of what Barbara Tye, in Chapter 2, calls the "deep structure" of schooling. When we look at demands on teacher time in that way and when we view them through the symbolic interactionist lens of "meaning," we are given a number of clues to the answer to our basic question, "What does it take to globalize the curriculum of a school?"

A Matter of Focus

During the CHI network project, the idea that teachers should be in their classrooms teaching continually was mentioned by many teachers and administrators. Even though teachers were attracted to the idea of sharing ideas with people from other schools, some teachers said they just could not leave their class(es) with a substitute while they attended workshops. In addition, some superintendents were reluctant to allow principals to declare a "minimum day" (early release of students) for staff development. In one case, a principal asked us to make the request because minimum days were just not done there. In that case, we obtained approval; but in another case we were told that the board of education did not want instructional time used for anything but instruction. The meaning of "school time" was clear in this district.

The notion that time should be used solely for traditional activity extended beyond the classroom. Early in the project, we attempted to have a two-day retreat in the nearby mountains for principals and selected district administrators. The idea had originated with the principals and was not part of our original understanding with superintendents. One superintendent was adamant in insisting that his principal was to spend his time at school and not at "out of town" meetings. We were quite successful, however, in having administrator meetings during the late afternoons or early evenings. On the other hand, because of negotiated contracts, we had no after-school meetings for teachers; and we were less than successful with the few voluntary evening programs we sponsored.

Six of the 11 network schools had a change of principals at one time or another during the four years of the project. Thus, we worked with a total of 17 principals. By classifying the responses of both principals and teachers to questions about principals' goals, we were able to determine if they used a (1) focused, (2) diffuse, or (3) coping style with regard to goals and the use of time to attain them.

Seven principals at four schools were focused. That is, they had a few, well-articulated goals that they pursued rather vigorously. At three of these schools, globalizing the curriculum, while not necessarily the highest priority, was clearly among the set of primary goals and, as a matter of fact, tended to get a fair share of staff time. At the fourth school, the original principal, while professing support for our project, was actually opposed to it, preferring what he called in a memo to a teacher "William Bennett's humanities approach." He was clearly focused on the development of a quality academic program for the top 10-15 percent of the student body. His time was spent on that program, and the school clearly obtained results. When he retired, he was replaced by a principal who also was focused and who included global education as a priority goal. The project, of course, fared better. Interestingly, in all six cases of principal change, the goal style (as opposed to goal content) of the original and replacement principal was the same for each pair.

Three principals at two schools had what we call a diffuse goal style. That is, they clearly articulated goals—but there were many goals, and time was divided accordingly. Our project was always well accepted by these principals and by several teachers at these schools. However, we always felt we would have done better if there had been a sharper focus on global education.

The remaining seven principals at five schools had what we call a coping goal style. They seemed to react to whatever came along and had many things going on at their schools. None of these principals ever purposely impeded the project. Generally, they complied with our requests for staff meeting time, release time for teachers, and so forth; but the project never really flourished at any of these schools. Teachers at these schools had a difficult time identifying the goals of these principals. When interviewed, they said such things as, "Getting through to retirement," "Making things look good," "Doing what the district wants," and "I really can't tell."

Much of the literature on educational change points to the principal as playing a key role. Jane Boston, in Chapter 5 of this book, discusses principal leadership. If we were to replicate the CHI project with the intent of totally accomplishing the globalization of the curriculum, we would want to select principals who had a focused goal style. We also would want to work hard to see that one major focus for the principal would be global education.

Global Education Extended

Additional Themes

Thus far, I have explored some of the themes that emerged from the data gathered in the CHI study in a network of 11 schools in southern California. That study was designed to explore the question, "What does it take to bring a global perspective to the curriculum of a school?" These themes are discussed further by B. Tye and K. Tye (in press).

The relationship between global education and multicultural education is one theme that emerged from the data. Much of southern California serves as a "gateway" for immigrants from Latin America, Asia, and other parts of the world. One of the school districts in our study served students who spoke 56 different languages. How to best teach in such a complex situation is a concern of many thoughtful teachers. We found several such people, particularly English as a second language (ESL) teachers, attracted early to our project.

Another theme that emerged was one we labeled "prevailing district ethos." From our data, we have hypothesized that the goal focus of principals is as much a result of such an ethos as it is a matter of individual personality. If the primary expectation of a principal is to meet the demands of the superordinate system, the principal will not assume a leadership role and set her own goals for the school. Rather, the principal will simply be a manager with a "coping" or "diffuse" goal style. Such expectations exist, to one degree or another, in all districts. At a time when site-based decision making is being put forth as an ideal, the question really is, "How can a district establish a climate that encourages creativity at the site level while, at the same time, it guarantees equal opportunity and maximum results in all schools?" As has been suggested, our data gave us some insights into this issue.

In our discussions at CHI of the "unique personality of a school," described by Barbara Tye in Chapter 2, we frequently pondered an issue we came to call "resilience." We worked with two schools (designated A and B here) with almost identical qualities. Grade spans were the same, as were the characteristics of the student populations, the faculties, and even the principals. And, yet, when we visited school A, we always came away with the feeling that there was little hope that anything good could happen there. Teachers were negative about the students. They didn't want to take on anything extra, including global education. To complain about almost everything was the norm. Simply put, it was an unpleasant place to be. School B was the opposite. With nearly the same conditions, people were "up," they seemed to like the students, and we looked forward to going there.

There is much written about school climate; and I believe that behavioral approaches to organization development can be successful. However, at times, even that is not enough. The history of these schools probably played a part in creating their climates. So did factors at the district level. A kind of self-fulfilling prophecy had set in. In school B, demographics had changed gradually over a long period of time. Faculty members had adjusted, and they felt they could deal with the situation. In school A, demographics had changed quickly, and faculty members had not adjusted. They were coping on a day-to-day basis. I do not believe that a problem-solving strategy would have worked here. There really needed to be confrontation, and we were not in a position to provide it.

Another construct we have used from social-interaction theory has been the "fitting together of professional biographies" (Lessor 1987). This process began for us when we first started looking for schools in which to work. We turned to superintendents or assistant superintendents whom we knew to be open to innovative projects or whom we believed to have somewhat of a global perspective. We then met with principals and teachers, and similar processes took place. In a couple of instances, we found people who were key to their setting, but who already had global education "staked out" as their personal territory. We were seen as threats, as not "knowing enough," or both. Needless to say, those people did not join the network we were establishing.

Many other themes emerged from the data. We do not have the space to discuss them all in this publication. However, one more does need to be explored: the interventionists themselves. During the CHI study, and with all of the limitations inherent in self-study, we did attempt to examine our own roles. We looked at such things as how realistic our workload was. A question we asked was, "How many schools can an interventionist-observer effectively work with?" We examined the adequacy of our skills and knowledge concerning global education and school change. We looked at our own feelings—frustrations, satisfactions, pains, joys; and finally, we charted what came to be known as "missed opportunities." These were times when, in retrospect, we felt we did not act when we should have, acted too late, or did act, but shouldn't have. For example, we probably could have worked more with some of the less goal-focused principals to help them see that globalizing the curriculum would have assisted them to accomplish a variety of their perceived goals; or we might have done a better job of linking together teachers who had similar interests across network schools.

In education, we spend a great deal of time discussing the faults and problems of "significant" others. Administrators talk about teachers, parents, and students; teachers discuss administrators, parents, and students; researchers look at all groups, also; and so on. We might do better if each of us spent at least a little time examining our own efforts.

Focus on Individual Schools

It has already been made clear that the CHI Network Project was guided by assumptions that call for educational change efforts at the local school level. Further, we have assumed that the mandating of new programs from superordinate levels actually can impede school improvement efforts. Interestingly, and even while this book was being written, school districts across the country, including Chicago and Los Angeles, adopted these assumptions and began to move toward site-based-management plans.

The authors of this book have made it quite clear that global education has the potential to serve as a catalyst for school improvement and renewal. Many schools have developed along these lines during the past few years and serve as models. Some of these schools, described by K. Tye (1990), include Adlai Stevenson High School in Livonia, Michigan; Decatur High School in Federal Way, Washington; Elaine High School in Elaine, Arkansas; Joshua Eaton Elementary School in Reading, Massachusetts; McClure North High School in St. Louis, Missouri; Miami High School in Miami, Florida; Northeast School in Monteclair, New Jersey; Park View School in Huntington Beach, California; Taos High School in Taos, New Mexico; and Tuffree Junior High School in Placentia, California. In addition, the American Forum is currently organizing a "model school network" in selected communities throughout the United States. The plan calls for the ultimate involvement of schools in ten school districts (Kniep 1989a).

For the person who might visit any school-based programs, the most important thing will be to ask the correct questions. For example, *Global Education: School-Based Strategies* (K. Tye 1990) discusses the preceding schools according to the following concerns:

1. An accurate picture of the setting at the beginning of the program (community, school, faculty, curriculum);

2. Insights into who or what caused the program to be initiated, including individual backgrounds and motives;

3. Comprehension of the leadership roles undertaken during the program by the superintendent, principal, and others; and

4. Knowledge of external support systems such as grants or linkages to colleges and universities.

With such background knowledge, the visitor to such a school is prepared to examine the actual program, comparing what was originally proposed with what actually exists and looking at problems that have arisen and how they have been dealt with. This comprehensive view of innovations is important because settings vary and ideas are not necessarily transferrable from one school to the other without significant modification. As pragmatists, American educators are so often bent on finding what works that they frequently overlook the fact that change occurs in a systemic fashion—when you change one thing, you affect others. The management of change requires that we anticipate and plan for systemwide consequences.

Need for Additional Research

In 1983, before the CHI project began, Barbara Tye and I conducted a review of the research in global education. We relied heavily on Judith Torney-Purta's (1982) seminal research review that she presented at the National Conference on Professional Priorities. We also examined a number of studies not covered in her report.

We concluded that the kinds of research in the field have developed quite unevenly. There was a good deal of what we labeled *developmental research*. Such research has a psychological orientation and deals with defining the appropriate age for teaching cross-cultural and cross-national awareness and appreciation. Much of this research is of high quality and gives good direction to practitioners if it is translated appropriately.

We labeled a second category *program research*. Studies in this category, too, can be said to be psychological in orientation because most use some type of experimental design. There was a dearth of such research; and as Torney-Purta noted, most of what existed was weak. Such studies usually purported to test the effectiveness of a particular curriculum or teaching method. There is need for much more research of high quality in this category.

We called our third category *research on change*. There has been a great deal of such research in education, in general. However, almost none of this work has been applied to global education, either in the sense of defining new studies or in the sense of giving guidance to practitioners. It was for this reason, and because of our backgrounds with change projects, that we chose to form the Center for Human Interdependence and to carry out the global education study directed at answering the question, "What does it take to bring a global perspective to the curriculum of a school?"

While our sample of schools was not large enough for our findings to be generalized to all schools, we believe that we have raised a number of significant questions and have begun the exploration of important themes with which global educators should become familiar.

A few other studies have begun to explore the relationship between global education and what we know about educational change. The American Forum project, Education 2000, has a sophisticated research plan that will involve the collection of baseline and process data, as well as several kinds of outcome data. It also includes the use of outstanding national research consultants and local research teams (Kniep 1989b). Another recently completed project of note, American Schools and the World, at Stanford University, included two case studies at sites where faculty members were attempting to develop global education programs (Duggan and Thorpe 1986).

We need much more research in this category in a variety of schools and schooling contexts—for example, networks, districts, and departments. Until then, we will operate from conventional wisdom and find ourselves at the mercy of trendiness and the whims of political ideologues.

175

Finally, we described a category of research we called *school-based research*, conducted by practitioners in collaboration with faculty members from colleges and universities or representatives of districts and intermediate agencies. Procedures for school-based research, also called action research, are as follows:

  • Selection of a specific problem and the formulation of a hypothesis that implies a goal and procedure for reaching it.
  • Careful recording of actions and procedures (accumulation of evidence to determine the degree to which the goal is reached).
  • Inferring generalizations from the evidence about the relation between the action and the desired goal.
  • Continually retesting the generalizations on other action situations (Bellack et al. 1953, Corey 1953).

For example, an elementary school faculty might be bothered by the fact that their students develop very little geographic understanding. There are three obvious alternatives in such a situation. First, the school can intensify its present efforts. Second, it can discard its present program and arbitrarily adopt a new one, risking an inappropriate solution. Third, it can create a program of action research.

If the school selects the third alternative, it initiates the steps suggested previously. Once the problem has been identified, a hypothesis is stated. For example, it might be hypothesized that if we infuse the existing social studies courses with geographic concepts recommended by the Joint Committee on Geographic Education (1984), then at the end of four years we will expect students to develop the heretofore missing geographic understanding.

Procedures for the program are established, and teachers are trained in their use. Records are kept on what is done, and concept development is measured over the four-year period. While standardized achievement tests are administered, they make up only a small fraction of the paper-and-pencil, observation, interview, documentary, and unobtrusive data that are collected.

At the end of four years, all the evidence is brought together; and tentative generalizations are stated. For example, it might be observed that when the recommendations are followed, both knowledge and concept development are better across the board, but some students do not appear to do better at geographic problem solving. Further analysis, however, might show that too much reliance was placed on reading from textual material and not enough on more active learning—such as planning various trips, simulations, computer linkages with schools in other parts of the world, and investigation of community economic connections with the rest of the world. Ultimately, an action research approach to instruction can reap great rewards in the form of improved programs. If the community is kept informed and appropriately involved at each step along the way, the odds are that community members will be both understanding and supportive of the changes (see K. Tye and Novotney 1975, pp. 88-90, for other examples of action research).

Need for a Global Perspective

This book set out to accomplish three purposes: (1) to explain, as clearly as possible, what global education is and why it is particularly important now; (2) to assist those who wish to develop their own global education program by describing how it works and how it can be implemented; and (3) to show how global education can serve as a vehicle for bringing about school improvement. The book was written for global educators to assist them with their efforts to promote the movement and for other thoughtful educators who might consider bringing a global perspective to their curriculums.

The rapid changes in today's world underscore the need for our young people to have an education with a global perspective, one that emphasizes the interdependence of the world and the need for cooperation. The development of a global perspective, however, has two major obstacles to overcome. First is the "deep structure of schooling," those pervasive shared values of society that determine what and how teaching and learning will occur; these values and perceptions often lag far behind the real needs of society. Second, some political ultraconservatives actively oppose global education because they see it as an attack on the particular kind of nationalism to which they are committed.

Despite these constraining forces, strategies are available to thoughtful people who wish to globalize the schools. Strategies include (1) developing local leadership; (2) involving the community; (3) creating partnerships between schools and other agencies, including colleges and universities; (4) turning to newer national curriculum projects that contain a global perspective; and (5) conducting more and better research, particularly action research and studies of school change. Most important, we have suggested the creation of opportunities for school-based improvement efforts in which teachers and others have time for thinking, planning, study, and personal development. Further, we have reported several programs that attempted to create such opportunities.

In examining these programs, we identified a number of themes that, in turn, have given insights into how a globalized curriculum can be brought about.

For a decade now our schools have been "marking time," victimized by political rhetoric and a preoccupation with less meaningful reforms. It is time for bold new action, again. The strategies suggested here—combined with a powerful concept, global education—can be used to develop the kinds of schools the United States needs now: dynamic, relevant, and oriented to the future. As Lee Anderson pointed out in Chapter 1, to do otherwise is to put at risk the children we love, the students we teach, and the nation we cherish.

References

Alger, C.F. (1974). *Your City in the World/The World in Your City*. Columbus: Mershon Center, The Ohio State University.

Bellack, A., S.M. Corey, R.C. Doll, M.F. Egdorf, B. Everett, and D. Fraser. (1953). "Action Research in Schools." *Teachers College Periodical*, 54:246-55.

Blumer, H. (1969). *Symbolic Interaction: Perspective and Method*. Englewood Cliffs, N.J.: Prentice-Hall.

Boyte, H.C. (1980). *The Backyard Revolution: Understanding the New Citizen Movement*. Philadelphia: Temple University Press.

Corey, S.M. (1953). *Action Research to Improve School Practices*. New York: Teachers College Press.

Duggan, S.J., and S.D. Thorpe, (April 20, 1986). "Obstacles to Global Education." Paper presented at the annual meeting of the American Educational Research Association, San Francisco, California.

Fullan, M. (1982). *The Meaning of Educational Change*. New York: Teachers College Press.

Goodlad, J.I., M.F. Klein, and Associates (1974). *Looking Behind the Classroom Door*. Worthington, Minn.: Charles A. Jones Publishing Co.

Gusfield, J.R. (1970). *Protest, Reform and Revolt: A Reader in Social Movements*. New York: Wiley.

Hanvey, R.G. (1976). *An Attainable Global Perspective*. Denver, Colo.: Center for Teaching International Relations.

Joint Committee on Geographic Education. (1984). *Guidelines for Geographic Education*. Washington, D.C.: Association of American Geographers and National Council for Geographic Education.

Kerckhoff, A.C. (1970). "A Theory of Hysterical Contagion." In *Human Nature and Collective Behavior: Papers in Honor of Herbert Blumer*, edited by T. Shibutani. Englewood Cliffs, N.J.: Prentice-Hall.

Kniep, W.M. (September 1989a). "Global Education as School Reform." *Educational Leadership* 47, 1: 43-45

Kniep, W.M. (1989b). *Education 2000: A National Model Schools Network* (Research Plan). New York: The American Forum for Global Education.

Lessor, K. (May 18, 1987). "The Theoretical Orientation of Symbolic Interaction and the Field Work." Unpublished manuscript.

Rogers, E.M. (1962). *Diffusion of Innovations*. New York: The Free Press of Glencoe.

Sherif, M. and C.W. Sherif, eds. (1967). *Attitude Ego-Involvement and Change*. New York: Wiley.

Torney-Purta, J. (May 1982). "Research and Evaluation in Global Education: The State of the Art and Priorities for the Future." Paper presented at the National Conference on Professional Priorities, Aerlie House, Virginia.

Tye, B.B., and K.A. Tye (in press). *Global Education: A Study of School Change*. Albany: State University of New York Press.

Tye, K.A., ed. (1990). *Global Education: School-Based Strategies*. Orange, Calif.: Interdependence Press.

Tye, K.A., and J.M. Novotney. (1975). *Schools in Transition: The Practitioner as Change Agent*. New York: McGraw-Hill.

Tye, K.A., and B.B. Tye. (January 1984). "Teacher Isolation and School Reform." *Phi Delta Kappan* 65, 5: 319-22.

Weick, K.E. (1976). "Educational Organization as Loosely-Coupled Systems." *Administrative Science Quarterly* 21, 1: 1-19.

About the Authors

Kenneth A. Tye is the editor of *Global Education: From Thought to Action*. He is Co-Director of the Center for Human Interdependence, Chapman College, Orange, California.

Charlotte C. Anderson is President of Education for Global Involvement, Inc., Illinois World Trade Center, Chicago, and Research Associate at the Chicago Teachers' Center, College of Education, Northeastern Illinois University, Chicago.

Lee F. Anderson is a Professor in the Department of Political Science and in the School of Education and Social Policy, Northwestern University, Evanston, Illinois.

James Becker is a Senior Consultant in the Social Studies Development Center, Indiana University, Bloomington.

Jane A. Boston is President of Global Educators, San Leandro, and co-owner and consultant, Boston Associates, Livermore, California.

Toni Fuss Kirkwood is a Global Education Specialist, Bureau of Education, Dade County Public Schools, South Central Area, Miami, Florida.

Steven L. Lamy is an Associate Professor of International Affairs in the School of International Relations, University of Southern California, Los Angeles.

Jan L. Tucker is Professor of Education and Director, Global Awareness Program, Florida International University, College of Education, Miami, Florida.

Ida Urso is the Executive Director of World Goodwill, an educational non-profit organization with offices in New York, Geneva, and London. She was formerly a Staff Associate with the Center for Human Interdependence, Chapman College, Orange County, California.

Barbara Benham Tye is Co-Director of the Center for Human Interdependence, Chapman College, and Chair of the Education Department, Chapman College, Orange, California.

ASCD 1990–91 Board of Directors

Elected Members as of November 1, 1990

Executive Council

President: Donna Jean Carter, Vice President of Corporate Affairs, Josten's Learning Corporation, San Diego, California

President-Elect: Corrine Hill, Principal, Wasatch Elementary School, Salt Lake City, Utah

Immediate Past President: Patricia Conran, Superintendent, Eagle County School District, Eagle, Colorado

Francine Delaney, Elementary School Principal, Asheville, North Carolina

Delores Greene, Assistant Superintendent for Elementary Education, Richmond Public Schools, Richmond, Virginia

Barbara Jackson, Executive Assistant to the Superintendent, District of Columbia Public Schools, Washington, D.C.

Edith Jensen, Associate Superintendent for Instruction, Lexington County School District 5, Columbia, South Carolina

Luther Kiser, Associate Superintendent for Curriculum and Instruction, Ames Community Schools, Ames, Iowa

Charles Patterson, Superintendent, Killeen Independent School District, Killeen, Texas

Arthur Roberts, Professor of Education, University of Connecticut, School of Education, Storrs, Connecticut

David Robinson, Superintendent, Sheridan Public Schools, Sheridan, Arkansas

Everette Sams, Professor of Education, Middle Tennessee State University, Murfreesboro, Tennessee

Arthur Steller, Superintendent, Oklahoma City Public Schools, Oklahoma City, Oklahoma

Review Council

Chair: Mitsuo Adachi, Professor and Chair, University of Hawaii, College of Education, Department of Educational Administration, Honolulu, Hawaii

Donna Delph, Professor of Education, Department of Education, Purdue University-Calumet, Hammond, Indiana

Benjamin Ebersole, Assistant Superintendent of Curriculum and Instruction, Hershey Public School District, Hershey, Pennsylvania

Carolyn Hughes, Assistant Superintendent, Curriculum and Program Development, Oklahoma City Public Schools, Oklahoma City, Oklahoma

Marcia Knoll, Assistant Superintendent, Valley Stream Central H.S. District, Valley Stream, New York

Board Members Elected at Large

Harriet Arnold, San Jose, California

Alice Bosshard, Director of Instructional Resources, Valdez City Schools, Valdez, Alaska

Rita Dunn, Professor, St. John's University, Jamaica, New York

Esther Fusco, Principal, Babylon School District, Stony Brook, New York

Sandra Gray, Director, Southwest Missouri State University, K-12 Laboratory School, Springfield, Missouri

Phyllis Hobson, Director, Parental Involvement Program, District of Columbia Public Schools, Washington, D.C.

David Jones, Jr., Director of Secondary Programs, Metropolitan Public Schools, Nashville, Tennessee

Ina Logue, Director of Curriculum and Instruction, Allegheny Intermediate Unit, Pennsylvania State University, Pittsburgh, Pennsylvania

Alex Molnar, Professor, Department of Curriculum and Instruction, University of Wisconsin-Milwaukee

Linda O'Neal, Mill Valley, California

Anne Price, Assistant Superintendent, St. Louis Public Schools, St. Louis, Missouri

Yolanda Rey, Director for Staff Development, El Paso Independent School District, El Paso, Texas

Susan Spangler, Director of Elementary Curriculum, Millard Public Schools, Omaha, Nebraska

Judy Stevens, Director of Elementary Instruction, Tomball Independent School District, Houston, Texas

Beverly Taylor, Director of Professional Growth, Curriculum Design for Excellence, Oak Brook, Illinois

Elizabeth Turpin, Principal, Lansing School District, Lansing, Michigan

Belinda Williams, Paterson Board of Education, Paterson, New Jersey

Hilda Young, Principal, New Orleans Public Schools, New Orleans, Louisiana

Affiliate Presidents

Alabama: Ed Hall, Assistant Superintendent, Talladega County Board of Education, Talladega

Alaska: Peter Larson, Professor of Education, Kenai Peninsula, Homer

Arizona: Larry McBiles, Deputy Associate Superintendent, Arizona Department of Education, Phoenix

Arkansas: Charles Russell, Fayetteville Public Schools, Fayetteville

California: Robert Garmston, California State University–Sacramento

Colorado: Roscoe Davidson, Superintendent, Englewood Public Schools, Englewood

Connecticut: Christine Roberts, Professor of Education, University of Connecticut, Storrs

Delaware: Hugh Ferguson, Shue Middle School, Newark

District of Columbia: Roberta Walker, Washington, D.C.

Florida: Margaret Baldwin, Director of Elementary Education, Hendry County School Board, LaBelle

Georgia: Robert Clark, Associate Superintendent, Marietta City Schools, Marietta

Hawaii: Theodore Nishigo, Likclike School, Honolulu

Idaho: Jerrie LeFevre, Assistant Superintendent, Mountain Home

Illinois: Richard Hanke, Thomas Junior High School, Arlington Heights

Indiana: Leo Joint, Assistant Superintendent of Elementary Instruction, Valparaiso Community Schools, Valparaiso

Iowa: Bonnie Benesh, Director of Curriculum and Instruction, Newton Community School District, Newton

Kansas: Larry Bowser, Assistant Superintendent, Seaman USD #345, Topeka

Kentucky: Caroline Pinne, Curriculum Resource Director, JCPS/Gheens Professional Development Academy, Louisville

Louisiana: Alta Brown, Covington

Maine: Phyllis Deringis, Division of Curriculum, Department of Educational and Cultural Services, Augusta

Maryland: Ronald Thomas, Division of Instruction, Baltimore City Schools, Towson

Massachusetts: Andy Platt, Action

Michigan: Edward West, Grand Rapids

Minnesota: Barbara Elvecrog, Roseville

Mississippi: Tommye Henderson, Coordinator of Staff Relations, Columbus Public Schools, Columbus

Missouri: Jolene Schulz, Director, Missouri Education Center, Columbia

Montana: Tim Sullivan, Butte

Nebraska: Martha Novak, Principal, Ralston Senior High School, Ralston

Nevada: Joyce Woodhouse, Partnership Office, CCSO, Las Vegas

New Hampshire: Ruthanne Barr Fyfe, Jaffrey Grade School, Jaffrey

New Jersey: Brenda Benson-Burrell, Glassboro State College, Glassboro

New Mexico: Elizabeth Posey, Coordinator, Instructional Cooperation, Region XIX Education Service Center, El Paso

New York: John Glynn, Principal, Central Senior High School, Valley Stream

North Carolina: Marcus Smith, Salisbury

North Dakota: Donald R. Emch, Superintendent, Flasher Public School District #39, Flasher

Ohio: Sharon Pierson-Zimmers, Vandalia Butler City Schools, Vandalia

Oklahoma: Ken Baden, Principal, Park Lane Elementary, Lawton

Oregon: Dean Thompson, Director of Curriculum, Umatilla County ESD, Pendleton

Pennsylvania: Jack Jarvie, Assistant Executive Director, Northwest Tri-County I.U., Edinboro

Puerto Rico: Etheldreda Viera, Professor, Catholic University of Puerto Rico, Ponce

Rhode Island: Donna Murphy, Director of Instruction, West Warwick Public Schools, West Warwick

South Carolina: James Buckner, Richland School District #2, Columbia

South Dakota: Lynn Davidson, Mitchell School District 17-2, Mitchell

Tennessee: Lana Doncaster, Director, Program Services, Tennessee School for the Deaf, Knoxville

Texas: William McKinney, Region IV Education Service Center, Houston

Utah: Ann Mayberry, Salt Lake City

Vermont: Raymond McNulty, Windham Southeast Supervisory Union, Brattleboro

Virgin Islands: Sandra Lindo, St. Thomas

Virginia: Walter Gant, Assistant Superintendent for Program Services, York County Public Schools, Grafton

Washington: Maryann Johnson, Union

West Virginia: Patricia Pockl, Wheeling

Wisconsin: Ron Lange, School District of Elmbrook, Brookfield

Wyoming: Robert Watson, Wright High School, Wright

Alberta, Canada: Arnold Ostfield, Edmonton

British Columbia, Canada: Owen Corcoran, Superintendent of Schools, School District #55, Burns Lake

Germany: Sandra Seto-Kuplinski, Assistant Principal, Ramstein Elementary School, Ramstein

Netherlands Antilles: Josianne Fleming-Artsen, Principal, Board of the Methodist Agogic Center, Philipsburg, St. Maarten

The Netherlands: Ruud Gorter, Director, Association of Educational Advisory Centers in the Netherlands

Singapore: *Ang* Wai Hoong, Chairman, Pro-tem Committee, Curriculum Development Institute of Singapore

United Kingdom: Barbara Graff, Special Education Specialist, DoDDS

ASCD Headquarters Staff

Gordon Cawelti, *Executive Director*
Diane Berreth, *Deputy Executive Director*
Frank Betts, *Director, Curriculum/Technology Resource Center*
John Bralove, *Director, Administrative Services*
Ronald Brandt, *Executive Editor*
Helené Hodges, *Director, Research and Information*
Susan Nicklas, *Director, Field Services*
Michelle Terry, *Director, Professional Development*

Francine Addicott	Vicki Hancock	Raymond Njoh
Teddy Atwara	Vonda Harlan	John O'Neil
Vickie Bell	Mary Harrison	Jayne Osgood
Kimber Bennett	Ned Hartfiel	Millie Outten
Robert Bennett	Dwayne Hayes	Kelvin Parnell
Sandy Berdux	Davene Holland	Jayshree Patel
Jennifer Beun	Julie Houtz	Margini Patel
Karla Bingman	Angela Howard	Yvette Pelt
Joan Brandt	Harold Hutch	Sydney Petty
Dorothy Brown	Arddie Hymes	Carolyn Pool
Garland Brown	JoAnn Jones	Jackie Porter
Kathy Browne	Mary Jones	Ruby Powell
Robert Bryan	Teola Jones	Pam Price
Colette Burgess	Mary Keen	Lorraine Primeau
Angela Caesar	Michelle Kelly	Gena Randall
Barbara Carney-Coston	Stephanie Kenworthy	Melody Ridgeway
Sally Chapman	Leslie Kiernan	Mickey Robinson
John Checkley	Lynn Klingler	Gayle Rockwell
RC Chernault	Lars Kongshem	Cordelia Roseboro
Eddie Chinn	Shelly Kosloski	Hank Rueter
Sandra Claxton	Terry Lawhorn	Beth Schweinefuss
Carrie Conti	John Mackie	Bob Shannon
Agnes Crawford	Indu Madan	Carolyn Shell
Elaine Cunningham	Lynn Malarz	Joyce Sparrow
Marcia D'Arcangelo	Joyce McKee	Valerie Sprague
Paula Delo	Anne Meek	Eddie Staats
Keith Demmons	Clara Meredith	Lisa Street
Becky DeRigge	Susan Merriman	Susan Thran
Gloria Dugan	Jackie Miles	René Townsley
Shiela Ellison	Ron Miletta	Dianna Vipond
Gillian Fitzpatrick	Ginger Miller	Judi Wagstaff
Chris Fuscellaro	Frances Mindel	Jim Warren
Sonja Gilreath	Nancy Modrak	Al Way
Regina Gussie	Cerylle Moffett	Scott Willis
Dorothy Haines	Carlita Nivens	Carolyn Wojcik